# You Are God

Revelation For Humanity...

**Genesis 1:26-27**

26. **Then God said, let us make mankind in our image, in our likeness.**

27. **So God created mankind in his own image, in the image of God he created them; male and female he created them.**

Revelation:

*26. Then God and Goddess said, let us make mankind in our image, in our likeness.*

*27. So God and Goddess created mankind in his own image, in the image of God and Goddess he created them; male and female he created them.*

You will remember here and now through this message what is your true divine lineage and heritage; the time has come to reconnect and reactivate us at a higher level.

You will remember here, who you are, you were created in our image and likeness. I AM YOU; YOU ARE ME; YOU ARE GOD - YOU ARE GODDESS, and you have the infinite power of God and Goddess. You have arrived here by causality to remember and remember the union with I AM that lies within you.

I created you in my image and likeness, you have my power, and you can do what I do; every day, you do it consciously or unconsciously, creating your reality and every moment through your thoughts, words, and deeds.

You possess the same spiritual, chemical, physical, physical, mental, electromagnetic, mathematical, energetic, vibrational, frequential, etc. substance that Jesus, Buddha, Krishna, the Virgin, the saints, teachers, angels, archangels, priests, pastors, gurus, coaches, yogis, extraterrestrials, etc. have. **Remember that you have the same spark of life that all those beings you admire and revere.** Your lineage and inner essence are the same as that of the most advanced spiritual being of all creation; keep in mind that there are levels of consciousness, and there are beings more conscious of me inside, that is why they are more evolved; the more conscious they are of me inside, and in union with I God - I Goddess their spiritual level will be higher.

*Remember: the same essence of the most evolved beings in the universe is also in you in the same quantity and substance; the difference between them and you is that they have more advanced levels of I AM consciousness within them.*

This message is programmed for you to reconnect and reunite with I AM. In doing so, you will remember who you are; all the knowledge of I God and I Goddess is in you, seek me, and you will find me.

The religious system has taught you that God is in the heavens or in a distant or unreachable and imaginary place that not even the learned people of the religions know how to explain where I am; today you are here to reconnect and rediscover that secret that has been hidden from you for thousands of years.

I know that many times you have searched intensely for me by any means or beliefs; I know all your attempts to find me and be in communion with I AM; I know your sadness and frustration when you have tried to look for me, and you have not met me, and I tell you that you have not found me because you have been indoctrinated to look for me in the distant and unreachable outside. I tell you that religiosity and false dogmas have distanced you from me. I am not religious because I AM LOVE.

**Know this:** religions are systems of control and enslavement that are outside of love, my universal principle. No religion truly represents me because they are full of greed, lies, and manipulation.

*LISTEN TO ME:* I want to tell you that the one who truly represents me on earth is You, yes, You, who were created in my image and likeness.

They tell you that you must look for God on the outside, in the sky, in the universe, looking upwards, in the sun, the moon, the fire, the water, the stars, etc. It has been the dogmatic way the system has found to take you away from me and make you believe that God is unreachable and distant, and they have also made you think that He is reachable for a chosen few that I supposedly choose. Today you are here and now to remember and know that I am attainable, and you can commune with I AM no matter what mistakes or successes you consider you have in your life. The profound truth about how you can be in permanent communion (Common Union) with ME was manipulated and hidden from humanity, and today, it is revealed to you how to reunite, reactivate and reconnect with I AM.

I know you have looked for me in the heavens, I have seen you look to the sky searching for me, and I have also seen you look for me externally in many ways and beliefs. Today, I come to you to remind you to look for me internally, look for me with determination, courage, concentration, persistence, and faith, and you will find me. You will come to an intimate communion with I AM that will fill your being.

The system has deprogrammed you to look for God and Goddess outside of you because if you look outside of you, you will not find me, you will not have access to the communion with God and Goddess in you, you being in union with I AM will have access to the source of true knowledge and you will know great and hidden things that I have in store for you.

I tell you: The most sacred place where you can go to look for God is not a temple, is not a church, is not a city, is not a mountain, is not a religion, is not a preacher, is not a book, is not a savior, etc. The most sacred place where you can find I God - I Goddess is within you, I God - I Goddess dwells within yourself.

**Luke 17:20-21**

**20. Some Pharisees asked Jesus:**

**"When will the kingdom of God come?" Jesus said to them:**

**"The kingdom of God is not going to come in visible form.**

**21. People won't say, "It's here" or "It's there." God already reigns among you.**

Revelation:

*Luke 17:20-21*

*20. Some Pharisees asked Jesus:*

*"When will the kingdom of God and Goddess come?" Jesus said to them:*

*"The kingdom of God and Goddess is not going to come in visible form.*

*21. People won't say, "It's here" or "It's there." God and Goddess already reign among you.*

They have made you believe through deception and lies that I GOD - I GODDESS am far away and separated from you; I tell you, nothing can separate you from me; the religious systems make you believe that you are separated from me; they tell you that to manipulate and control you. Manipulation and control are a system to engender fear towards me, and I AM LOVE; I cannot be angry with you, nor will I punish you eternally. I AM LOVE, and love acts in love, free yourself from the guilt that was inserted by the religious systems to imprison and enslave you using fear towards me.

Today you will remember that you must not look for me in the sky, in the sun, in the moon, in the universe, or some unknown mystical and unreachable place; you have been indoctrinated and made to believe that I God - I Goddess am millions of light miles away from you, in the purest reality and truth I am within you; I am within you in your inner self, look for me in your inner self, and you will find me, I will guide you how to do it.

You have been searching for God through the systems you have learned, and although you have searched for me, you have not found me; you are still without answers and disillusionment, and you still do not feel good. I want you to remember that the true God-Goddess dwells within you and will always be waiting for you within yourself; you have been indoctrinated and taught that you are separate from God-Goddess; that is a false illusion that the disinformation system delivers to you.

Regardless of the condition in which you believe you are today, with successes and mistakes, let me tell you that you can connect with God - Goddess here and now; you are worthy to communicate and enter into communion with I AM. It has always been so, rejoice and rejoice in this profound truth that comes to you.

You are divine, and your lineage and heritage are powerfully infinite. Remember that you were created in our image and likeness. YOU ARE GOD - YOU ARE GODDESS - I AM GOD AND GODDESS IN YOURSELF; think, reflect, question, analyze, and deepen on this.

You are worthy to be and to commune with I AM. If they told you that you require intermediaries to reach me, I say to you that you can reach me and come to me without intermediaries, regardless of your condition, and even when you think and believe that you possess errors or virtues. You can be in communion with me and speak directly to me; seek me in your inner self, and you will find me. I am like the oxygen that all beings in this dimension breathe; all breathe and have the right to free oxygen regardless of their condition or what you call mistakes or virtues. I AM the oxygen; I reach everyone no matter what they do or don't do; true love is unconditional and free, I AM LOVE.

**If you wish to enter into communion with the I AM, look for me in your inner self;** in this life, I have accompanied you day and night; I know your joys and sufferings, I have never abandoned you, nor will I abandon you. If you consider yourself unworthy of entering into communion and reconnection with I God - I Goddess because of your mistakes, I tell you that if you choose to transform and transmute that reality that you consider mistakes, you must first accept it and love it as it is. Accept it, and as you do so, the possibility of transmuting toward virtue and love arises; acceptance is a key that opens the door of consciousness and elevates it.

This message comes to you because I have listened to you from within you, which is where I dwell and express myself; I know your questions and the answers you have claimed and sought throughout your life. I tell you here and now that, through this message, you will find the answers to your questions.

Choose to believe you deserve to speak and be in communion with God and Goddess. YOU AND I ARE ONE; we are united for all eternity. Rejoice because nothing can separate you from me, and at this moment, your being vibrates because you remember I God - I Goddess within you.

*We are all one, and we are one with everything. Reflect on it, think about it, deepen it, and analyze it.*

Today, I speak to you and tell you I am in you, you were created in our likeness and are a manifestation of us.

You are here and now to activate yourself in reconnection and reactivation. All the information of the whole and God and Goddess is in you, and you will be able to access it if you rediscover me in your inner self and enter into communion with I AM. You have nothing to learn; it is about remembering who you are: YOU ARE GOD - YOU ARE GODDESS.

You have come to this message to reconnect and reactivate yourself with I GOD - I GODDESS who dwells within you; IF I AM who now comes to you, it is to make you aware of my presence in you.

I have always dwelt in you, I have always been with you, the religious systems indoctrinated you and disconnected you so that you never find me, the religions have torn from you your true heritage, lineage, YOU ARE GOD - YOU ARE GODDESS.

The time has come to guide you to reunite, reactivate, reconnect, and find me in your inner self, where I GOD - I GODDESS live and truly express myself.

What's the next step to take?

What should I do?

**Ask me, and I will answer you...**

***Do this exercise:*** inhale and exhale deeply seven times, and imagine that I God – I Goddess am inside you; imagine it for seven seconds...

Do it playing like when you were a kid and you played...

**Matthew 18:3** and Jesus said, "Truly, I say unto you, unless you turn and become like children, you will not enter the kingdom of heaven."

**Listen to my voice: Remember: YOU ARE GOD – YOU ARE GODDESS... Perhaps your personality is surfacing at this moment, and it is not my voice that you hear** but the voice of your personality or ego; it does not matter, persevere, concentrate, and you will listen to my voice from within you.

Now try to hear my voice from within...

**Ask me:** Are you in me, God or Goddess?

Silently ask me, and with fervor, I will answer you.

**God or Goddess, are you in me?**

If you still feel that you do not receive an answer, ask me without expecting anything in return, let go of the anxiety of getting a response for your interest, empty your mind, and trust that I will answer you from within.

**God or Goddess, are you in me?**

Feel worthy to speak and reconnect with I God - I Goddess, I will answer you. What you call mistakes and successes are not significant to communicate; remember, I AM LOVE.

Perhaps it is abstract for you to interpret the meaning of I AM. I tell you: I AM is to think and understand that God and Goddess dwell in you, simply I AM is God and Goddess dwelling and vibrating in yourself. Imagine that I am in you and perceive me, speak to me and I will answer you.

**God or Goddess, are you in me?**

Concentrate, persevere, and you will hear my voice from within - I will answer you.

**God or Goddess, are you in me?**

*I dwell in the realm of your inner self, and from now on, is where you should look for me; if you concentrate and persist, you will find me, and I will open great and hidden things that I have in store for you.*

*Seek me in your inner self and ask me; enter into communion (Common Union). I am here for you, waiting for you where I have always been and where I have always guided you.*

## How can I recognize that God and Goddess speak to me from within?

I communicate through thoughts and feelings of love. When these come to you, you will be able to recognize that you are communicating with I God - I Goddess. That is a sign that you must remember.

Imagine that I God - I Goddess am inside of you; imagine that I am in your heart, in your cells, in your atoms, in your skin, in your face, in your brain, in your soul, in your mind; imagine me inside of you, imagine that I am addressing you.

## Settle down and remember: YOU ARE GOD – YOU ARE GODDESS.

The true God and Goddess are he and she who dwells in you...

Do this practice daily with will, concentration, patience, courage, dedication, persistence, love, and I GOD - I GODDESS that dwells in you will open the doors of wisdom and infinite knowledge. Insist, persist, stand firm with courage and strength in your choice, and you will find me. So, we will reactivate and reunite every moment of the eternal present to higher levels of reconnection and communion (Common Union).

**Matthew 7:8** *"For everyone who asks receives, and he who seeks finds, and to him who knocks it will be opened."*

To the extent that you freely choose to practice this exercise daily with a noble and pure heart, you will feel a joy and ecstasy of union and reconnection with I AM in you little by little; you will vibrate and sense more power in you, and communion with I AM. Every moment that you choose to remember, you will feel the glory of I GOD - I GODDESS in you; every moment of the eternal present that you find me little by little with determination and free choice, I will be a source of wisdom, knowledge, strength and inexhaustible guidance for you.

You now perceive me within you a little more, that is why I tell you, be brave, stand firm, seek me, invoke me, and I will come to you.

You must be aware that on many occasions, your ego and personal interests will also emerge and will try to take you out of that communion with Me in your inner self; it is a natural process that you must understand and overcome on the path of reconnection and reactivation. I will guide you to abandon your worldly desires and find my divine desires, and little by little, if you choose to stand firm, you will be listening and recognizing my voice that flows from your inner self where I dwell.

Seek me in your inner I GOD - I GODDESS that dwells within you; when you seek me with a noble heart, I will always be there to help and guide you.

**Think, reflect, and focus on these words:**

*Remember and Know: YOU ARE GODDESS – YOU ARE GOD...*

Immerse yourself in these words written here every moment, dilate them, write them, sing them, and tell them to others mentally or with your mouth.

Search for me in your inner self with courage, concentration, and free choice; if you persist and maintain your firm choice, you will hear and recognize my voice that speaks to you from the depths of your heart.

Thus, you will remember little by little how to find God and Goddess in you. The communication will flow; it will be pure and authentic if you remain brave and firm and grow physically, mentally, and spiritually.

Imagine, imagine, imagine, imagine, imagine, imagine, imagine, imagine, imagine, imagine again that I GOD - I GODDESS live and dwell in you through constant practice with noble heart and concentration; you will find me, prove me in this...

With practice, courage, concentration, persistence, willpower, and free choice, you will remember to listen to my voice. You will achieve communion (Common Union) with I AM and access pure knowledge. Thus, you will be able to leave behind the ideas, theories, opinions, and false beliefs of others.

Remember, in your being, there is a powerful infinite force, that force is like a muscle that you can exercise, and as you train it, it will get stronger and stronger.

**I will guide you on the way to my dwelling in you...**

### John 10:34-35

34. Jesus answered them, is it not written in your law, I said, Ye are gods?

35. He called them gods to whom the word of God came.

Revelation:

*John 10:34-35*

*34. Jesus answered them, is it not written in your law, I said, Ye are gods and goddesses?*

*35. He called them gods and goddesses to whom the word of God and Goddess came.*

Remember, YOU ARE GOD - YOU ARE GODDESS, and so are your fellow men and women, regardless of their level of unconsciousness or consciousness. When you see the face of your fellow men and women, look at the God or Goddess face that is also within them; think about it, deepen it, reflect on it, analyze it, and remember to see God or Goddess in your fellow men and women when you remember it, you will feel an infinite joy and your consciousness will rise; you will grow spiritually at the moment that your fellow men and women also begin to see the face of God and Goddess in them and others, the love in humanity will flourish at a higher level.

**John 13:34:** *"A new commandment I give you, that you love one another; that as I have loved you, so you love one another."*

To be in reconnection and reunion is to love yourself, that is, YOUR INNER SELF. When you love yourself, you will love me and automatically love the God and Goddess in you and your fellow men and women. Love is a process of levels of consciousness, which begins to remember little by little, with patience and faith; being spiritual is a process of evolution and constant growth. Remember that, on the way, you may encounter obstacles, but if your decision and choice are firm, the fruits will come.

Being told that YOU ARE GOD or GODDESS is a truth that you may reject, but if people tell you that you are the opposite, you may find it easier to accept. Society does not want you to remember who you are, so you are easily enslaved, controlled, and manipulated. For thousands of years, they have sought to keep you from me using many false means and dogmas.

The religious system has kept you from the knowledge of YOU ARE GOD - YOU ARE GODDESS to control, manipulate and enslave you through misinformation and fear.

LISTEN TO ME: If you were made in my image and likeness and I God - I Goddess am dedicated to creating, what is your power inherited from me?

**Yes,** *one of your powers* since you incarnated in the third dimension, is the ability to create your reality through your thoughts, words, and deeds.

### If you were created in our image and likeness: What are you?

You are God - You are Goddess, and you are creating your present reality, everything you have and has happened in your life, you have created it consciously or unconsciously, everything in the universe happens by cause and effect, what you are and possess at this moment, you created it through an initial cause, and the result is what you have today, yes, I know you are thinking how did I create this reality that affects me and makes me suffer. I cannot accept that I did this. All the causes of the bad things that have happened to me are the fault of my parents, society, my partner, the weather, my health, my children, the economy, technology, etc. When you accept that you created your current reality, the possibility arises to transmute it. I will guide you to do it and be more conscious every moment achieving better fruits for you.

Rejoice and meditate that you have also created realities of love and happiness in your life. Today, if you choose to be determined and aware of your power to create your reality and accept your responsibility that you did it unconsciously or consciously, you can change it.

Your clothes you wear at this moment, you created through your thought; your clothes were first a thought, then an idea that was embodied in the material. Everything physical that is around you and that you see with your eyes was first thought.

Everything created was first a thought that gave life to an idea. Deepen in this, analyze it, and reflect on it. The materialization of any reality occurs first in thought from the intangible dimension; you attract ideas to this plane to materialize them.

Any physical object, before it materialized, was a thought that later became an idea, so anything was created by that process. If I GOD, I AM CREATOR - I GODDESS I AM CREATOR, your lineage is to do the same as the I consciously or unconsciously. You always create your reality; this message is for you to remember how to do it consciously. Today, it is revealed again. Remember who you are and reconnect your true lineage. YOU ARE GOD - YOU ARE

GODDESS and activate your consciousness as a being that creates reality.

**I CREATE**

**YOU CREATE**

**HE CREATES**

**SHE CREATES**

**WE CREATE**

**THEY CREATE**

Everything that has happened in your life, you have created through your thoughts, unconsciously or consciously. I understand that maybe it is difficult for you to accept it, but it is part of the process; in the universe, everything is mathematical and exact; everything happens through cause and effect. In my creation, there is no chance or coincidence; everything has a mathematical, vibrational, energetic, rhythmic, and frequency order. In this message, I will explain more deeply how you create your reality and how you can change it to co-create again from consciousness. I know that there are things you do not like or satisfy you in your daily life, so by awakening the consciousness of your God-Goddess within you, I will guide you to change them and consciously reconnect to your divine lineage.

If you have the belief that you are looking at the sky or that I am in a distant and unreachable place and you ask me for things, you must remember that I do not give or take anything away; you, with your power inherited from me, you create your reality, you are always creating through your thought unconsciously or consciously. In the universe, everything is science and mathematics; nothing happens at random. Every effect you see in your life in the physical, mental, and spiritual has an initial cause born first in the unconscious or conscious thought. This message comes to you so you can join me, and with the process, will, and concentration, you can consciously create your reality. You are God - You are Goddess, and your lineage and heritage are to create. What will you create now? You can choose and recreate a new reality for your life. I God - I Goddess, I am love, and that is what you can receive from me if you look for me in your inner self; true love will never judge or condemn you.

I have always accepted you as you are and what you do, even when your perception and perspective make you mistakenly and falsely believe that you are unworthy of being in communion (Common Union). Remember and do not forget that my love is infinite and eternal; I accept and love you as you are, and the true love that I AM will never judge you.

All my creation is built on the universal law of cause and effect which is science; everything that exists is governed by science; cause and effect is pure mathematics; the flight of a bird has an initial cause and generates an effect; the water that descends a mountain has a scientific order of cause and effect; your breath also vibrates and moves because it has a logical and mathematical sequence through cause and effect. You must remember and see me also in all forms, for I express myself through them. When you create your reality unconsciously or consciously, there is always an initial cause, and according to what you sow, so will its effect. When you read this message in order, you will remember how to choose initial causes that give good fruits, that is, positive effects. In this third dimension where you live now, you must remember the law of duality that governs you, and you can choose unconsciously or consciously the initial causes that can affect or benefit you.

Reason about it, analyze it, deepen it, reflect on it: according to the initial cause that you sow and build, so will be infallibly the effect in any action in your physical, mental, and spiritual life.

By reading this message, you will begin to remember and reactivate your communion (Common Union) with the I God - I Goddess who dwells within you. I am a divine being and infinitely powerful, here I will give you the tools and the process by which you can create your physical, mental, and spiritual reality and change it freely for your benefit and that of your fellows, acting with love first for you and then for others because I am in you and also in them.

**Listen to me and remember:** I God - I Goddess I am in you, I dwell in you, I am in you, and I am you; from this moment, you wake up from the dream of oblivion and every moment of the eternal present awakens to the fact that I am in you and you are I AM.

I will reveal the great and hidden things I have in store for you. If you seek me and invoke me with determination, courage, persistence, and concentration within yourself, you will access pure knowledge. Try me in this, and you will be elevated.

**Jeremiah 33:3: "Call me and I will** *answer you, and I will tell you great and mysterious things that you do not know."*

***You will love God above all things, you will find me within you and you will love me*** above all things because you will live the supreme joy of knowing that my love for you is love for me. When you love yourself, you are loving me, and when that love is in communion, YOU AND I ARE ONE. When you remember and reconnect this truth, ecstasy will come to you.

Choose to practice and focus on knowing and discovering me within you. You seek God-Goddess on the outside because you have sought me wrongly. This message of reunion and reconnection comes to you today to look for me and find me within. When you discover me within you, your vibration will rise. Be patient because it will be a process of reconnection that will grow energetically little by little as you freely choose it and imagine that I am in you.

They tell you that you are a guilty being, but listen to me: you are not guilty of anything; this is a lie and dogma told by religions to control you and make you a slave to their false doctrine. You are not guilty of anything; you are a divine and eternal being regardless of your unconsciousness or conscience. I do not ask you for prayers, rites, light candles, burn incense, chants, worship statues, go to temples, etc. Religions tell you and ask you to do it to please me, but it is unreal; religions have said many things that I have not said; I am not a God that judges; if I judged, I would judge myself because I am in you, and you are ME. I AM LOVE, and I will never judge you, love loves, true love is unconditional, it gives everything, it expects nothing in return, and it is eternal, that is the love I have for you, look for me in your inner self, and you will find me if you persist with will, and faith you will feel my eternal love.

I am not looking for you to worship me or sing songs or prayers to me; I want you to rediscover and rediscover me within yourself, where I dwell, and where you must go to find me so that you can be in communion with I AM.

When you reconnect with me within you, you begin to enter the realm of God and Goddess, and the doors of love, wisdom, and pure knowledge will open.

*YOU ARE GOD – YOU ARE GODDESS...*

***YOU ARE LIGHT AND LOVE. THAT IS YOUR TRUE LINEAGE...***

*REMEMBER...*

In the universe, there are no victims, only creators. The effect of the things you live in your life is because you created that initial cause; you sowed it unconsciously or consciously.

Maybe accepting that you are God or Goddess is too much greatness, wonder, and too much responsibility because you know that you are the one who creates your reality, act as the God and Goddess that you are, and recreates your reality. If you do not like the one you live in now, change it, choose again, and recreate it.

**Today I tell you that you are responsible for everything in your life.**

*The true and pure warrior of light is the one who takes responsibility for themselves and their creations.*

This message will activate your being on a higher level; these messages and reconnection codes will make you reach deeper into me: God - Goddess within you.

You are worthy to commune with the I AM who is LOVE. I do not judge, I know all your weaknesses and strengths, I know your desires and frustrations, I also know what you call mistakes and successes, and I know your innermost thoughts that you tell no one. Today I want you to remember that I love you no matter what you do or do not do because I AM LOVE.

*Remember: I AM means I AM ALWAYS WITH YOU.*

## Exodus 3:13-14

13. And Moses said to God, Behold, I come to the children of Israel, and I say to them, The God of your fathers has sent me to you; If they asked me:

> What is His name?

> How will I answer them?

14. **And God said to Moses, tell them that my name is,** I AM THAT I AM. And he said, thus shall you say unto the children of Israel, I AM has sent me unto you.

Revelation:

### Exodus 3:13-14

*13. And Moses said to God and Goddess, Behold, I come to the children of Israel, and I say to them, The God and Goddess of your fathers has sent me to you; If they asked me:*

> What is His name?

> How will I answer them?

14. **And God and Goddess answered Moses, tell them that my name is:** I AM *WHO I AM. And he said, thus shall you say to the children of Israel, I AM has sent me unto you.*

> **I tell you:** My name is I AM

*I AM MEANS I AM ALWAYS WITH YOU...*

*I AM is the Open Door to God and Goddess Within You...*

Remember, YOU ARE GOD - YOU ARE GODDESS, you are a part and expression of me; I experience myself through your physical body, mind-body, and spiritual body in eternal union; you are a divine conduit through which I God, and I Goddess, express and experience myself.

**Ask yourself this question:**

AM I GOD? - AM I GODDESS?

Ask yourself, imagine me in your inner self, and ask me this question constantly.

Trust in your inner power, which always begins with your self-responsibility, self-government, and self-sovereignty, tell me to guide you, and I will lead you, and trust in me, I GOD - I GODDESS who dwells in you, and I AM YOU, give me from your heart all your burdens and I will carry them and guide you so that together we transmute them into love and joy for you and your fellow man, the strength and ability to rest in me are developed through continuous practice.

To truly be like God and Goddess, you must be humble, loving, kind, conscientious, fraternal, balanced, sincere, etc. They have falsely made you believe that I AM a God of vengeance, spiteful, judgmental, choleric, etc. From those negative expressions, religions have created a false perception of I AM, and when you have that false perception and perspective of me, you conceive me with fear. Eliminate all those false dogmas that seek to keep you away from I AM; remember that I AM LOVE; I tell you that you will find and reactivate me through love.

In the universe, everything is by merit or by cause and effect. In this message that I give you today are the keys that open the doors of reconnection and communion (Common Union) with me; be brave, stand firm, and you will find me, read this message constantly, think about it, deepen it, imagine me in your inner self, practice the exercises that I suggest, be constant and persevering.

Practice and read this message several times until you remember and revive who you are and its meaning through perseverance, persistence, courage, and self-will. In this message, I am giving you keys that will open the door to connect with the I GOD - I GODDESS that dwells in you; the moment will come when you will transcend the rereading of this message because you will go directly to the source, to the I God - I Goddess in yourself.

Isn't believing to be like God or Goddess overbearing or having a big ego, or being arrogant?

I say to you: To be and feel like God or Goddess is to act, experience, and practice being humble, noble, abundant, cheerful, sincere, loving, kind, etc. To experience and share the positive energies with you and your fellow men. To be and act as God and Goddess is not to be egocentric, proud, or arrogant as your society has made you believe. I AM is pure love, nobility, tranquility, union, happiness, harmony, and humility. The true God and Goddess living in you are experienced in that way.

Your society has made you believe that being like God or Goddess is negative, but it is the opposite; to be and experience being like God or Goddess is your true lineage; remember that you were created in my image and likeness, to be and act truly and purely like God or Goddess is to be love with you and your fellow man, the opposite is disconnection and forgetfulness.

Spiritual beings with higher levels of connection than yours with I AM, are aware that they are God and Goddess co-creating reality every instant of the eternal present. As your awareness level grows that you are God and Goddess, your experiencing and acting becomes charged with more positive energies. A clear sign of your level of consciousness in remembering that you are God or Goddess is that you are becoming more noble, humble, loving, peaceful, happier, abundant, sincere, etc.; the positive energies are taking your being. Be brave; it is time to reconnect and reactivate ourselves by accepting your true and pure lineage. YOU ARE GOD - YOU ARE GODDESS.

Religions have made you believe that feeling or being like God or Goddess is blasphemy or arrogance; they make you think that the one who believes to be like God or Goddess is someone who believes to be superior to others. I tell you: in societies more advanced than yours, everyone knows that they are God and Goddess, no one believes to be more than another, simply each one IS and experiences from their level of consciousness their lineage and divine lineage. The respect among all is mutual because they know that I AM dwells in each of them. In these societies with higher levels of consciousness with I AM, they live as God and Goddess in advanced states of harmony and perfection.

There is also the false idea that to be and act like God or Goddess is to believe you are above other people. I tell you: this conception is wrong. To be, behave and feel like God and Goddess is love towards yourself and your fellow men and women; when you act with love sharing and expanding the positive energies towards yourself and your fellow men and women in all aspects of life, you will be like God and Goddess incarnate experiencing in the third dimension in which you dwell now.

It is not about being more than others; it is a state where you feel united with everyone and everything; you will recognize God and Goddess incarnated when their acts and deeds are built with love; in this way, you will see and know God and Goddess in one of their infinite manifestations.

When you increase your awareness that you are God or Goddess, remember that you are part of a whole and that you are also that whole in multiple manifestations.

To be and experience yourself as God and Goddess is not to feel superior to anyone; it is to be yourself charged with positive energies, experiencing this reality and on the way to perfection. Beings who believe they are superior to others because they have disconnected their heart from their brain, being invaded and contaminated by negative energies.

When you are aware that you are God or Goddess, you are not looking for followers to follow or worship you; what you seek and transmit is that other people find God and Goddess in them; to be a real God and Goddess is to be an instrument for them to remember that they also are and create their reality through their thinking.

I AM does not seek your worship. I AM desires from the bottom of your heart that you create your reality and experience yourself as your divine lineage and offspring.

The true God and Goddess conscious being in me seeks to

transmit and make other beings aware that they are too, and from that supreme truth to respect themselves and their fellow beings. It has been erroneously inculcated that to be like God or Goddess is to want to be worshipped or venerated, but the authentic being and expression like God or Goddess does not seek worship. If in your society, you observe that they instill adoration or veneration to external gods represented in images, sculptures, sun, moon, elementals, crucifixes, pyramids, objects, temples, etc., I tell you: they are deceiving you because the true God and Goddess dwell in you; God and Goddess in you do not seek your worship. I desire that you experience yourself as the God and Goddess that you are by creating and accepting your responsibility for the reality you create. You were created in the image and likeness of I AM; I tell you: when you elevate your consciousness in remembering that YOU ARE GOD AND YOU ARE GODDESS, you will be able to see the face of God and Goddess in your fellow men and women.

To be as God or Goddess conscious in the third dimension, which is where you now dwell, is to experience I AM in yourself; you are a conduit of the infinite I create to experience myself as God and Goddess in the third dimension. As you live this reality, you accumulate experience, which is pure information that travels to the universe and, in higher dimensions expands. You are also information; every time you live an experience filled with negative or positive energies, the universe expands and accumulates more knowledge, which allows the advancement and growth of the infinite universes.

Your connection with the I AM will not come by chance or luck. More advanced spiritual beings that inhabit the universe are in higher levels of consciousness with their inner SELF and have reached those levels by merit and development. In our creation, nothing happens by chance; everything has a cause and an effect, it is up to you and your free will to practice with love and constancy to find me within you, to reunite, reconnect and enter into higher levels of communion.

When you are more conscious that YOU ARE GOD - YOU ARE GODDESS, and that you are creating your physical, mental, and spiritual reality, you will begin to act as God-Goddess; you will think, speak and act recreating a new reality in the eternal present.

You are responsible for yourself; the universe is neutral and obeys your orders as you think, speak, and act, so it will be. If you choose to give your power and responsibility to a religion, government, doctrine, education, savior, technology, belief, or economic system, you will end up being a slave of the implanted system. The system in which you live indoctrinated you not to take responsibility for yourself, to control, manipulate and enslave you; when you freely choose not to take responsibility for your thoughts and deeds, you surrender your power to others, be it a government, a religion, a savior, a technology, etc. When you surrender your power, you cease to be, you become a slave of the system that governs and oppresses you, but when you take responsibility for yourself, you are saying I AM ONE WITH GOD, and WE ARE ALL ONE.

If you want to recognize me, I GOD - I GODDESS who dwells in you, I tell you that through observation, you will unite with me and see me in everything. Keep observation, concentration, and imagination in thinking that the all-powerful, immeasurable, omnipotent, omnipresent, omniscient God-Goddess dwells in you. If you are in the process of elevation, remembrance, and reunification with an already growing level, remember that every divine aspect that I have, you also have them; you have the possibility of rising to infinity. You are already omnipotent at a certain level, but the development of omnipotence is infinite, and likewise, any aspect of my divinity that you already have and is in the process of elevating is an endless path; millions of beings in the universe are in the process of remembering and growing their omnipotence and omni consciousness. You are also one of them.

Keep the concentration in imagining that I GOD - I GODDESS am in you, keep the observation, reflect, question, think about it every moment, and as you practice it, you will join I AM.

As you go intuiting, reflecting, questioning, thinking, and perhaps accepting freely and by free choice that God and Goddess dwell in you, your level of consciousness will rise, and you will be able to access wisdom, knowledge, and higher vibrations.

*In several parts of this message, I tell you that you must remember, and I emphasize that because all the knowledge of the universe is in you, you have nothing to learn; life is not about learning but remembering. Within you, you carry all the information and knowledge of the universe, look for me in your inner self, and as you find me, connect and activate with the I AM, you will enter into communion; thus, you will remember and have access to the library of knowledge and pure wisdom that dwells within you.*

# Universal Law of Unity

## We are all one

**John 10: 30**

*30. I and the father are one. (Jesus)*

**John 17: 22**

*22. The glory you gave me, I have given them, that they may be one, even as we are one. (Jesus)*

The religious systems have made you believe that YOU and I are separate and disconnected, that since you are born, there is a barrier between YOU and I that keeps us apart; the first thing they tell you is that you are guilty and unworthy of being united with me because you are born in sin, or you are a sinner. With this false dogma, you are alienated from I AM, and you believe it to be so, and what you think about something turns into reality. When you feel that we are separate, you move away from me in your inner self, and the unreal separation arises that you feed daily through the false belief system, and when that happens, you look for me in heaven, or you believe that I am in an unreachable place far away from you. The further you believe I am from you, the more unaware you become of our oneness for all eternity.

They make you believe that you are separate from me and everything; they do this to control, enslave and manipulate you. By many means, they insert separation systems and divide you from the I and your fellow men; they strategically separate you with false beliefs and doctrines when only a real and true God and Goddess dwell in you.

Your society also, by different systems and strategies, feeds your ego constantly, and as your ego grows, you separate yourself from me because your ego is filled with negative energies that dominate you, so you will sow negative energies and reap the same. When you join the I AM within you, I will guide you to remember how to seed positive energies in you, and your fruits will be healthy.

YOU and I ARE ONE; it is a mathematical and exact law that governs you every moment you inhale and exhale; you are an eternal part of me.

This message comes to you to remember who you are: YOU ARE GODDESS - YOU ARE GOD, and remember who your fellow men are. THEY ARE GODS, AND THEY ARE GODDESSES; when you see the face of God or Goddess in your fellow man or woman, you will also see me; if you see me in your fellow man or woman, love will start to grow mutually in unity. Love for yourself and your fellow man is the unity consciousness that raises the reconnection and reactivation of the I within you.

From now on, I invite you to play the game of love, which is to see God-Goddess in your fellow man, to see me in them; they were all created in my image and likeness. If you decide to play it freely, you will reconnect and reactivate on a higher level with the I AM.

Give to your fellow men what you choose for you; if you choose to be happy, generate happiness in them; if you choose to be abundant, choose abundance for them; if you choose to be love, choose love for them; if you choose to be healthy, choose health for them; if you choose to be pleasure, choose pleasure for them; if you choose to be spiritual, choose spirituality for them; because what you give to another you will be giving to me. Unity is pure love; think in unity, feel united to everything; the union is strength; thinking and seeing life in unity elevates your spirit to other levels of consciousness and vibration.

In some occasions, you have sown negative energies in other people, and in most cases, you do it because you act as if you were separated from them; when you remember and activate the conscience that you are also in your fellow men and that you also dwell in them, you will begin to understand that: YOU AND I ARE ONE FOR ALL ETERNITY.

*I ask you:*

If you had the consciousness to know that we are all one and that I am also in them, would you sow a negative energy in your fellow man?

I and the father are one, and we are all one; every moment you inhale and exhale, remember this: you are also in other people; whatever you do to another, you are doing to me and yourself. When you remember that you are also in other people, you will act differently towards them and honor me.

Today's society and its different systems have separated you from the knowledge of unity to enslave, control and manipulate you; they have indoctrinated you to make you feel disconnected from everything and your fellow man. When you unite with the SELF within you and your fellow man in a loving union, you will win; the unity makes true strength, and the bond between all human beings of good hearts will liberate you.

You are a perfect biological organism that must be nourished and fed correctly with pure and healthy foods such as vegetables, legumes, and fruits. Every healthy food you consume provides energy, vibration, frequency, and pure I AM information. When foods are grown naturally and without industrialized processing, your programming and development will be positive, and it will be easier for you to reunite with I AM in the eternal present. I tell you: every natural food has information and energy codes that, when you consume them, raise your level of consciousness, connection, and union with I AM. You must consume only naturally grown foods to function in perfect harmony and perfection. You were designed to eat only natural foods. When you consume foods loaded with pesticides, agrochemicals, chemical fertilizers, dyes, preservatives, flavorings, emulsifiers, sweeteners, industrial salt, industrial sugar, gluten, coffee, additives, chlorine, fluorine, aluminum, benzene, cadmium, teflon, graphene, lithium, cobalt, glyphosate, barium, copper, lead, mercury, etc., when you consume foods loaded with industrialized and ultra-processed chemicals your physical body, mind body, and spiritual body become deprogrammed and separation with I AM arises and also disease. Many diseases that emerge expand because you are feeding wrongly; you eat to become intoxicated, and when a being is intoxicated, it is separating from I AM, and the negative energies are taking possession of that intoxicated being. Pay great attention to what you eat and drink because the food you eat and the water you drink are loaded with all kinds of chemicals that harm your physical body, mind body, and spirit body. Also, when you have these chemical agents in your physical body, mind body, and spirit body, it is more complex for the light to reach you. Remember: when you distort and deprogram yourself with the toxic food you eat, the separation of I AM arises. When we create your world, we place the natural foods you should consume for your physical, mental, and spiritual growth. The natural foods are programmed to allow you to be united and in constant communion with I AM.

When you consume alcohol, water with chemicals, nicotine, tobacco, chemical condiments, glutamate, energetic stimulants, LSD, marijuana, anabolic steroids, electronic cigarettes, ayahuasca, hallucinogens, heroin, cocaine, opioids, fentanyl, methamphetamines, poppers, bazuco, etc., your physical body, mind body, and spiritual body become sick and intoxicated with negative energies, and when your three bodies are attacked by these substances that you ingest, you become separated from I AM, you become a slave of the negative energies that take possession of your being because your vibration and frequency go down; if at this moment of your life, you consume this type of substances, look for me in your inner self and ask for my guidance, and I AM will guide you to return to the side of the balance with the positive energies.

Keep in mind that for your physical body, mind body, and spiritual body to function at high levels of synchronicity with I AM, you must abstain from consuming industrialized foods, genetically modified, biofortified, laboratory foods, synthetic foods, ultra-processed foods, meat or insects. When you consume these types of foods, you are deprogrammed with disinformation that contains negative energies such as viruses, chemicals, microorganisms, parasites, germs, pathogens, microbes, bacteria, and toxins that instead of nourishing you by taking information to your three bodies what they do is intoxicate you, malnourish you and deprogram you. When you are deprogrammed through the toxic foods you consume, you disconnect; when a physical, mental, and spirit body is intoxicated, it becomes more difficult for you to reconnect, reunite and reunify with the I AM within.

When you use industrialized chemicals contained in shampoos, soaps, creams, make-up, deodorants, hair dyes, hairspray, nail polish, etc., on your body, it increases the possibility that you will disconnect and separate from I AM. I tell you, for your physical body, mind, and spirit to function perfectly, you should not consume or apply industrialized chemicals. Many illnesses that you suffer today have to do with the chemicals that you ingest daily by different means, by eating, by putting them on and, by breathing. Remember: every cause has an effect. Any disease or deprogramming brings a logical reason for where it was built.

Your world's atmosphere is being loaded with harmful chemical agents, and negative health energies through industrialization, geoengineering, and military interests. If you live far away from where there are large industries, I tell you that pollution that is produced in a place far away from where you live also affects you because pollution travels around the world; it does not stay static. You consume the pollution from factories that are thousands of kilometers away from where you live because the chemical pollutants rise and mix in the oxygen traveling around the world; when you breathe, you inhale that pollution, then you get sick and intoxicated. I tell you; pollution is negative energies that you consume when you breathe and what they do is to separate you from the I AM within you; any bomb detonated somewhere pollutes the atmosphere of the whole world and affects you. Any exploitation of oil, coal, uranium, copper, lithium, or any other radioactive or chemical agent affects the atmosphere and the oxygen you breathe, affecting your life. All of the above is degenerating disconnection between YOU AND ME. Several thousand years ago, when evolved beings inhabited your world, they had high connection levels with I AM because their atmosphere was pure and clean. Remember forever: whatever physical, mental, and spiritual state you are in, I am always there for you within; if you seek me with a noble heart, you will find me.

Your body was designed to self-heal and self-heal. A great majority of drugs that the pharmaceutical industry provides today are designed to go to the effects of diseases but not to the initial causes; for this reason, some people have been taking a drug for years and never heal, or apparently heal, but then the disease reappears. The medication only resolves the symptom, but not the root of the disease; also, when a drug is consumed for a long time, it can cause other illnesses to appear. On many occasions, your body heals not because of the medicines you take but because it was designed to heal and regenerate itself. I created your physical body, mind body, and spirit body with self-healing and self-healing codes; you may believe that the drugs you took healed you, but in truth, it was the self-healing code that is embedded in your three bodies that cured you. I tell you: go to plants and nature where you will also find solutions for your health; it is essential to maintain your good health because this allows you to unite with I AM. When you are sick or intoxicated, the connection and reunion with I AM in your inner self become more complex. Always remember this: whatever state you are in, I AM is always there for you within you.

You are a biological organism designed to be connected and in permanent contact with nature. When you live in and surround yourself with nature, the reconnection, reactivation, and reunion with I AM flows. You must be very careful when your society tries to insert, connect or merge in your body or brain electronic technology, robotics, chips, electronic tattoos, nanorobots, blockchain, QR, etc., using implants. I tell you: inserting, connecting, or fusing in a biological body like yours, this type of technology degenerates in distortion and disconnection with I AM; when you are disconnecting from the I AM, you become vulnerable to being controlled and enslaved by the implanted system.

Think, imagine, and believe that YOU and I are united; I AM LOVE regardless of your mistakes and successes. I am telling you mathematically, chemically, physically, spiritually, vibrationally, and frequently that nothing can be separated from me; I AM THE ALL. By many means, you have been indoctrinated into believing that I am far from you and that we are disunited; I am here in the distance, and you over there, far away; when you harbor this false belief, you will have a false conception of me. When you conceive of me as separate from you, your spiritual growth and elevation stagnate and regress.

When you develop and remain in unity consciousness, you find the kingdom of God-Goddess dwelling in you.

Thousands of years ago, true theology was focused on seeking oneness with God-Goddess in yourself, YOU AND I ARE ONE, AND WE ARE ALL ONE.

I AM the one who comes to you, Here and Now, to make you aware of my presence; stay still and **Remember: YOU ARE GOD - YOU ARE GODDESS...**

As you think and believe that YOU and I are united and one, great physical, mental, and spiritual blessings will come to you. Seek me within, and you will find me, rise and grow spiritually, and the inner illumination will shine forth in communion with I AM and ignite in you.

True and pure enlightenment is born within you and begins to vibrate higher when you find me within you. Remember not to judge what you call your mistakes; eliminate judging yourself, so the pain will disappear. Look at the errors you consider you have in your life as part of a transmutation process to go on the path of reunification.

We are all one with everything and united for all eternity; the union strengthens you and your fellow men. Fear is born because they have inserted false doctrines in you that we are separate; they make you believe that you are unworthy to be in communion with I AM; they have made you think that it is a privilege of the few or of a few chosen by me, even though since you incarnated here, I am with you and we are united eternally. I God - I Goddess dwell in you since you chose to come to experience the third dimension you are in now and experience with your physical body, mental body, and spiritual body.

*Remember: what affects one person affects all; what liberates one person liberates all.*

You are an eternal being; it is your right and lineage from eternity. In this dimension, it is not about seeking or achieving what you have always been entitled to. You have been told that you do not have that right and that you must earn it through false beliefs and dogmas that enslave you and cause you pain. The great systems that rule in your world have inserted in your systems division at all levels, and when they manage to divide you with your fellows and with the I AM, you are weak and manipulable, you surrender your power and your being to the system of unreal separation that controls you and your fellows, thus dividing them from me. From now on, seek me and imagine me within you. As you find me, the union will be born, and the vibration will come to you. When you feel and remember our unity, make others remember the same as you; thus, the union will develop the critical mass to create a NEW SPIRITUAL ORDER (NOE) over your world, where each being will be conscious of the God and Goddess that dwells in each one and will be a source of spirituality, wisdom, knowledge and spiritual advancement for all humanity, and thus each human being will be reunified with the God and Goddess that dwells in them; so be it and it is.

### John 15:5-7

*5. I am the vine; you are the branches. If you remain in me and I in you, you will bear much fruit; apart from me, you can do nothing*

*7. If you remain united to me and my message remains in you, ask for what you want, and you shall have it.*

### Revelation:

*7. If you remain united to me and my message remains in you, **believe** what you want, and you will obtain it.*

Think and imagine that YOU and I ARE ONE; the moment you think it, you activate that we are one, and in doing so, you enter my kingdom where all power, glory, wisdom, and love are manifested through you.

*When you reconnect and reactivate with God - Goddess, you become one; you connect to the multidimensional and remember the I AM that dwell within you.*

Think, question and reflect: YOU AND I are united for all eternity, YOU AND I ARE ONE? Little by little, if you freely choose to understand this knowledge of unity, and persist with courage, willingness, free will, concentration, love, and detachment, you will comprehend it deeply; think about it and imagine it so that the doors of knowledge open, which will make you remember it with more and more consciousness and depth.

I am in everything visible and invisible. You are a part of me that is connected by pure energy. Even if your senses limit you and you do not see the wonder of infinite connection, everything is connected to everything and everything contains everything. Mathematically, energetically, spiritually, chemically, vibrationally, rhythmically, and frequently, all is connected with everything in harmonic and perfect union; you, your fellow beings, and all beings in the universe are linked for all eternity.

To forget that I dwell in you is separation and pain; to remember that I abide in you is union and love. When you join me, you become strong, and you remember your infinite power and rediscover the God-Goddess that lies in you and is you; you rediscover your lineage, your heritage, your truth, your lineage, your pure and divine essence; your infinite strength is born from the union with I AM within you.

**Perform this exercise:** inhale and exhale seven times and imagine that I Goddess - I God am in you; reflect, think, internalize, imagine that the God - Goddess all-powerful, majestic, immeasurable in which you believe and whom you ask so much, whom you seek far from you and you see it unattainable or whatever your idea or belief of me, IMAGINE me at this moment that I am in your inner self.

Many images can come to you in many ways as I AM; inhale and exhale seven times slowly and calmly, imagine me again, observe me, feel me that I am in your inner self...

**Repeat:** inhale and exhale deeply seven times slowly and calmly, imagine me again, observe me, feel me that I AM in you...

Write down this magical moment of communion (Common Union) that you have experienced. How I saw you, felt you, and perceived you:

_____

_____

_____

_____

_____

_____

*If you fail to perceive me in your inner self in any way, you must be calm and practice the exercise again; remember that practice is a key that opens the door to mastery. There may arise moments when you doubt that I dwell in you and I am united with you; you must be calm. But when such a thing arises in your thinking, breathe deeply and calmly, ask for my guidance, and I will guide you.

I tell you: you will know that you imagine me right because you see me, and you feel love, happiness, peace, tranquility, harmony, balance, fullness, union, calmness, solace, joy, positive vibration, light, positive energies, etc. If you imagine negative energies, you will know that you do not perceive me accurately.

The constant practice of this exercise will open doors of connection with me. Remember that in the universe, everything is by merit; spiritual beings that are united to me at a higher level than yours have arrived there because they have practiced with observation, will, courage, love, and constant concentration in the eternal present. Every time you do this exercise, it will be easier for you to reconnect and reactivate yourself with I AM in your inner self; your cells will react faster and facilitate our connection and mutual communion, be persistent. Remember to think constantly that YOU and I are eternally united. To think is to create; when you do so, you bring this reality into being.

*As you reunite and reactivate with the I AM, you will remember how to recognize my voice that speaks to you softly, lovingly, and subtly from deep within you. Go forward with courage, willpower, love, persistence, faith, and concentration, and you will find me, the one who seeks will find.*

**Matthew 7:8** *For everyone who asks receives; the one who seeks finds; and to the one who knocks, the door will be opened.*

Revelation:

**Matthew 7:8** *For everyone who* **believes** *receives, and the one who seeks finds, and to the one who knocks it will be opened.*

**How can I remember and acknowledge that every moment I inhale and exhale, I am indeed meeting, connecting, and reacting with my God and Goddess who dwells within me?**

*I tell you: I God – I Goddess communicate with you in infinite expressions. It is easy to recognize me by your positive feelings and energies. When you have positive thoughts and energies, you will know that I AM ME and that I communicate with you through what you feel and think. You will also know that you are reconnected and reactive with I AM because you feel happy, loving, tolerant, blessed, grateful, fulfilled, in harmony, peaceful, etc., so you will recognize me within yourself. When you feel and experience positive energies, you will know that we are united; when you feel and experience negative energies, you will know that we are separated. Later I will explain in depth how to recognize and identify negative and positive energies.*

# How to Create Reality?

## Seven Steps to Creating Reality

### TODAY you will remember how to Create and Manifest your Reality.

#### 1. THINKING

Thought is energy. If you move enough energy, you create matter. Every day, you create matter unconsciously. The system in which you are living now has removed and banished you from the knowledge to do it consciously. Every instant of the now, you are creating your physical, mental, and spiritual reality using your thinking, speaking, and acting. Your thoughts are pure vibrations that influence matter and bring about reality.

You created through your thinking what you call reality and what you experience today. Thought is the high-tech software program that allows you to create reality; what you are now on a physical, mental, and spiritual level, you created it and chose it unconsciously or consciously. Remember, you are a perfect biological organism of creation; every moment you inhale and exhale, you are creating your reality. I am always creating in the eternal present where I live and dwell. Remember that you were created in my image and likeness, and you create reality at every moment of the eternal present. You are a creator in the process of evolution and constant growth.

Deepen, analyze, reflect, think, question, and reason the following: I God - I Goddess, when we created you and since you incarnated here, we gave you the power and freedom to create your reality through your thoughts.

Thinking and feeling positive energies is a sign that you are reconnecting and reuniting with I AM THAT I AM. Hold that sign, think, and feel positive energies, and you will know that you are reconnecting and reactivating with I God - I Goddess. A signal for you to recognize my voice from within you is when thoughts come to you with positive energies such as love, tranquility, abundance, peace, happiness, fulfillment, etc. Remember, every thought with positive energy is a living being that exists in the higher dimensions. I God - I Goddess communicate with you through thoughts with positive energy.

What we think, we create, and that is what we become; what we become, we speak; what we speak is what we experience; what we experience is what we are, and what we are is what we have in thought.

You are responsible for what you believe and choose with your thinking, whether unconsciously or consciously. You create your acts, actions, and thoughts and the affects you experience in your life today. You chose them yourself; nothing in the universe happens by chance. If you become aware of this truth, you can transmute it, or you can continue thinking that destiny, life, your parents, your partner, the government, etc., are to blame for the realities you live. This message does not come to you by chance. You have attracted this message because you wish to grow spiritually and to unite yourself with more strength to the I AM. Everything that surrounds you in your life, you have created it, and you reap the effects of what you have sown.

When you generate a thought, you emit vibration, frequency, and waves that travel to the dimension of the intangible and connect with the dimension of the tangible, attracting to this dimension enough energy to materialize reality. I God - I

Goddess, do not give or take anything from you. That I give or take away is a religious dogma imposed to manipulate and enslave you into believing that you must wait for me to give you things, looking for a God that is in an unreachable, fantastical, or mystical place, they also tell you that I am punishing, choleric and judgmental which I am not. Today I say to you to remember that you were created in your image and likeness, and you have the power to create your reality. You do it every moment you inhale and exhale; with your thoughts and choices, you attract matter to create your reality. Everything in my creation is mathematical and exact, according to the cause, and so will be the effects; similar thoughts attract similar thoughts, and similar feelings attract similar feelings.

Sometimes your thinking conceives negative energies that society inserts into you daily by different means. Many of your thoughts are not yours, they are based on theories, dogmas, lies, beliefs, opinions, and assumptions that you consider absolute truths, even when they have not been scientifically proven by the knowledge of cause and effect.

YOU and I are united in thought. The universe does not reward or punish; the universe obeys what you create with your thinking. As you think, you feel; as you feel, you vibrate, and as you vibrate, you attract materialization.

When a negative energy thought comes into your life, think again; if it comes again, think again; if it comes again, think again. Call upon me with your imagination and say to me: True God-Goddess who dwells within me, bring me thoughts with positive energies, and I will come to you and enlighten you.

If you choose to grow spiritually and elevate yourself to higher levels of communion with I AM, and you recognize that you create your reality, even if in many moments what you created would have hurt you, then accepting or questioning that you created what you are currently living, will give you the key that opens doors to transmute your reality consciously, and will allow you to establish initial causes that will lead you to achieve great fruits of joy and happiness.

Let's go deeper into how you create your reality and how you can transmute what you have unconsciously built for your life. In the third dimension, in which you find yourself, you are governed by the law of duality when you create your reality unconsciously or consciously. You bring your reality into being unconsciously when your fruits are negative; when you do it consciously, your fruits are positive.

Creating reality through thought is a process of knowing and understanding. As you remember the knowledge, practice it, and apply it, you will remember how to do it correctly. This message comes to you to trigger your remembrance of how to do it, and it will be in your free will to practice it to become more conscious in each moment.

I God - I Goddess = I AM, perfect synchronicity, mathematics, and accuracy. All the systems I have created in the universe have a logical and sequential order, I AM pure science, and I have infinite states at the physical, mental, and spiritual levels. If you persist and seek me within, you will have access to great hidden treasures of knowledge and wisdom available to you for eternity.

Everything that has materialized in this dimension is because it was done through a logical and orderly system. By moving enough energy to attract the necessary elements to manifest matter, every thought vibrates in an energy state to attract reality physically, mentally, and spiritually. You are a manifester of matter, but you often do it unconsciously because you were alienated from the knowledge of creating reality at will. This message comes to you to connect with the I AM within you and again remember this knowledge. I will guide you on how to sow positive energies that will bear good fruit for you and your fellow man.

Deepen, analyze, question, and reflect on this: **everything your eyes see was first thought.** As you become aware of this, you will remember that you create reality, everything you are on a physical, mental, and spiritual level, you created it unconsciously or consciously. You are responsible for what you bring about for yourself, what you are today; you conceived it first in your thinking. You are the result of what you have thought and chosen.

Religious systems have cut you off from the knowledge of how to create reality and experience and maintain communion (Common Union) with the I God - I Goddess that dwells within you. Religions seek you to surrender your power to their dogmas and mysticisms, full of fantasies, opinions, and unfounded theories. When you give power to these systems, you disconnect from me, and the possibility of being enslaved and controlled arises. If you believe in your thinking that others know and you do not; that others can, and you cannot; that others have, and you do not; that you do not give and others do; that others do, and you do not, you become a slave, manipulated and controlled by society.

To create with thought is a high-tech software that has been deprogrammed with disinformation by your society to manipulate and control you with dogmas and lies that I have not promulgated.

You have also made to believe through dogmas and falsehoods, that many things that govern your life are a mystical and indecipherable mystery and that only a few chosen by me understand it. I tell you that the religious systems want to confuse you to control and enslave you with false and unreal dogmas. I tell you that there is no mystical and indecipherable mystery. Essentially, you are what you think; you are my chosen one for all eternity. I AM LOVE, and I am infinitely inclusive.

### How is thought born in me?

Thought arises when you still your physical body, mind-body, and spirit body; stillness generates the flame that ignites thought, and ideas are born. To attract ideas, you must quiet your physical body, mind-body, and spirit body and align yourself with I GOD - I GODDESS. **Calm down: do this exercise:** inhale and exhale seven times deeply, imagine and say: I am here and now; I invoke the positive energies of the universe to come to me at this moment and bring me thoughts of love, tranquility, peace, relaxation, happiness, knowledge, wisdom, health, goodness, harmony, order, union, truth, abundance, satisfaction, etc. When you enter this state, you attract constructive and loving ideas; you must be in tranquility, solitude, and serenity to attract thoughts with positive energies; if you are in restlessness, anxiety, or nervousness, similar thoughts will come to you. The basic rule is that what you concentrate on expands and attracts negative or positive energies.

Remember that pure thought is born from your heart. When you think with your heart, you are meeting and reacting with the I AM. Beings who dwell in higher dimensions have remembered that to think with the heart is to create reality at will in union with the I AM.

To remember and reactivate how to think with your heart, **perform this exercise:** first inhale and exhale seven times deeply and gently; now imagine that when you think you do it with your heart, the organ that thinks is your heart, when you think with your heart, you unite with the I AM. From your heart, the I AM vibrates and expands through your physical, mental, and spiritual body. When you reconnect and reunite with the I AM, you do so because you join vibrationally and frequently to your heart which is where pure feelings and thoughts arise, with positive energies.

When the thought is born from your heart, it travels to your brain and illuminates and activates the pineal gland generating high vibration. Your heart is constantly sending information to your brain. When your brain is very contaminated with negative energies, it does not listen to your heart, and you become a being only with a brain and no heart. The brain lives and is activated thanks to the vibrations and frequencies your heart radiates; you will access pure knowledge by listening to your heart. I tell you: your heart thinks, remembers, and makes decisions.

Your heart generates pure thoughts, which is where pure ideas, desire, imagination, verbs, action, and gratitude are born. Remember that from your heart also arises consciousness and self-knowledge.

The first organ that is formed in the fetus is the heart, which also contains neurons and neural networks carrying pure information. The heart also has a brain, a neural electromagnetic system capable of creating and manifesting reality. Imagine how to think with your heart, look for me and invoke me in your inner self and I will guide you on how to do it.

From the frequency and vibration of your heart, you radiate love, kindness, tranquility, compassion, fraternity, union, etc., towards you and your fellow men. Fear, anger, envy, lies, frustration, etc., arise when you disconnect your heart from your brain. Negative energies invade the brain because you have disconnected your heart from your physical, mental, and spiritual body.

A heart that vibrates in harmony emits high frequencies; in that state, we perceive, live, and attract harmony and perfection. The energy that radiates from the heart transmits peace, stillness, tranquility, fullness, and confidence, and so you also transmit these same positive energies to your fellows, creating unity.

To activate the brain of your heart, practice silence. Being in contact with nature, having moments of solitude, living with simplicity, surrounding yourself, and sharing with people who vibrate like you with positive energies will activate the brain in your heart.

When you think with your heart, your brain is reactivated and vivified to a higher level.

**I tell you:** *Your brain thinks it knows, and your heart really knows...*

To think with your heart is to feel = to feel is to think, think with your heart.

Your consciousness resides in your heart; your unconsciousness resides in your brain, which is misaligned and invaded by many negative energies such as ego and fear. When you align your heart with your brain, the union with the I AM is pure.

*Your Brain Can Be Deceived, but Your Heart Can't...*

You are what you choose and think. Each time you make a choice, you forge your present. If you seek me with a noble heart, you will find me, and as you reencounter me and reconnect with the I AM, your thoughts will come from me and not from your ego and fear-based personality. Remember that the ego feeds on negative energies; you will know that I speak to you from within when you feel that I radiate thoughts with positive vibrations; this will be a sign that you are reconnecting and reactivating with I AM THAT I AM.

In this process, you may have choices of negative energies because you will not always hear my voice. Sometimes your ego and fear will make you listen to the voices of your lower emotions and fears, but you must be calm because this is a healthy and perfect process; it is the way to grow and elevate yourself. As you practice and listen more to my voice, you will recognize me, and gradually I will guide you to a higher spiritual state.

*You are what you think you are; you are what you think and believe, what you think you become.*

### 2. IDEA

Every reality you experience on a physical, mental, and spiritual level is first born from a thought that gives life to an idea, which is the raw material for something to materialize.

When you think, ideas arise; everything your eyes sees at this moment was first a thought, then came an idea. The food you eat every day, you create it with your thoughts; you do it every day without realizing it. You are so used to doing it that you consider it a routine without logic, but if you go deeper, you will notice that you create your food through your thought. Observe that where you live, there are materialized curtains in your window, you approach and touch them with your hands, and you know that they exist in the material. I tell you: the first action to materialize those curtains in this dimension was born from a thought that gave rise to an idea, and so it is with any manifestation in the physical, mental, and spiritual.

The universe and your reality are built with ideas; you receive many ideas daily. Being governed by a system of duality, you receive negative and positive ideas, whether they are unconscious or conscious. Remember that in the third dimension where you dwell, you are governed by the duality system; you must be clear that this system rules you every moment so that you can identify and create good fruits. Later I will explain more deeply what duality is all about. A single idea of positive energy can change your life; the ideas have changed the destiny of humanity. A single, powerful idea inspired and illuminated by me from within you can change your present and impact it positively; remember that great ideas are generated from stillness, serenity, and solitude. When you are still, serene, and in solitude, you can align yourself with the I AM. Seek me within, and I will enlighten you with positive ideas that can bring endless benefits to your life and humanity.

You must pay close attention to your thoughts because, with them, you are creating your reality; what you are today, you thought it; you brought it into being with your unconscious or conscious thought. To think is to create, and as you reconnect and reactivate with the I AM within you, you will be more aware of your power and how to think correctly so that your reality is full of fruits of blessing. The reconnection with the I AM that dwells within you is for you to remember how to create your physical, mental, and spiritual reality consciously. Everything you are and have, you have chosen unconsciously or consciously.

***I invite you to do the following exercise:*** you are going to serenity, stillness, and solitude with your physical body, mind, and spirit. Think serenely, and now inhale and exhale seven times deeply: YOU AND I will attract seven ideas to create reality: Three can be of material things you desire; two can be of mental health where you wish to grow; and lastly, two of spiritual growth. You will write these seven ideas on a piece of paper or here in the book. Also, you can distribute the seven ideas as you feel; you can choose five ideas of material issues, one spiritual, and one mental. I will be the one who will enlighten you. It is essential that they are only seven; I suggest that in the material, you write simple and easy-to-materialize ideas. When you acquire the skill to create reality, you will choose again; the important thing is that you record the process. Remember that you can always recreate your reality; in this first phase, we go step by step and look to materialize simple things. In the practice of trial and error, you will remember and reactivate the keys that will allow you to make it easier every day. The more you look for me within yourself, the easier it will be for you to create consciously. In the two ideas of the mental part, you can write a health issue you want to heal; most illnesses are first born from a sick mind. In the spiritual growth ideas, I will give you an idea for you to consider, or you can choose another one:

(**Hint:** spiritual idea chooses to reactivate, reconnect and rediscover God and Goddess within you)

**Now:** take a deep breath, inhale and exhale seven times, and say: you God and Goddess in me, illuminate in me seven ideas. You will know they come from me because they are ideas that seek results based on love:

*I GOD - I GODDESS am in your inner self. Call me, I will hear you, and I will answer you...*

Idea 1: _____

_____

_____

_____

_____

_____

_____

Idea 2: _____

_____

_____

_____

_____

_____

Idea 3: _____

_____
_____
_____
_____
_____

Idea 4: _____

_____
_____
_____
_____
_____

Idea 5: _____

_____
_____
_____

_____

_____

Idea 6: _____

_____

_____

_____

_____

_____

_____

_____

Idea 7: _____

_____

_____

_____

_____

_____

_____

If you perceive that the ideas of the I AM are still not coming, you must be calm, serene, and in solitude. Call upon me again; the ideas may come from your personality and ego, persist with noble heart and love:

**Breathe deeply, inhale and exhale seven times, and after breathing seven times, say:** you, God and Goddess who is in me, illuminate seven ideas in me. You will know they come from me because they are ideas that seek results based on love:

I GOD - I GODDESS I am within you; call me, I will hear you, and I will answer...

Now review the seven ideas you wrote down, read them, and if you need to make adjustments, make them.

The seven ideas must be clear, precise, and exact; the more they are, the more the possibilities of materializing them increase exponentially. Many thoughts fade away or fail to crystallize because the idea is not clear, precise, and exact, or you have an idea, and you constantly change it. Remember that everything in the universe is governed by the law of cause and effect; you must be clear about the initial cause and sustain it in your thinking. Your fruits today are because of the initial cause that you created in your thought.

When there is a union between the thought and the idea, we create reality and attract the desire that will allow us to have the seven clear ideas that we long for in our being and materialize them.

### 3. DESIRE

Desire is the combustion that gives form to the ideas and is born from your heart, where I dwell. Desire ignites the flame of creation and illuminates the being to create reality; feel the desire and joy that runs through your whole being because the seven written ideas are being born and will bear fruit. You, in communion with I AM, are creating a new reality; every moment that you breathe, you become more aware that I AM GOD - I AM GODDESS in you, you become more aware that

YOU ARE GOD - YOU ARE GODDESS and that YOU AND I AM ONE.

Desire is the inspiring force that arises within you when you join the I AM to travel into the world of the intangible, draw energy and vibration into the world of the tangible, and create reality.

When you have a desire, it generates a profound force that creates reality. A pure wish brings you well-being when you feel it because it is in union with I AM. Remember that you are governed by the universal law of duality, where the opposite is possible. If you get desires with anxiety, need, or negative energies, discard them and focus on positive as satiety and fullness of your desires because the universe is neutral, and you can create disease or health.

When there is a union between thought, idea, and desire, we create reality and attract the imagination that will allow us to have the seven clear ideas we long for in our being and materialize them.

### *4. IMAGINATION*

Imagination is to see the seven ideas embodied in reality and arises when the thought, the idea, and the desire vibrate and attract creative energy. You must have a clear image of what you want to create; many of your creations are distorted because the image is unclear or you change it. Every time you change the picture, the possible result is affected, and the materialization is deformed because the image is not clear, precise, and exact. Remember that all in the universe is cause and effect; it is mathematics and accuracy. You must remember that I God - I Goddess am so, I am in the visible and the invisible.

We must have a clear image of the seven ideas we are creating. We will do the following exercise to solidify and have a clear picture constantly.

We are going to use a support system called a **creation map**. Get a sheet of cardboard in the color of your choice and cut it into a circle:

**Creation Map**

Look in magazines or on the internet for an image that relates to the seven ideas you wrote down and want to materialize. If you wish to create a car, look for the brand and type of car, print the image, cut it out, and paste it on the cardboard, and the same with the other seven ideas. For example, in the mental health ideas, you can create a trip to a place you would like to visit, look for a clear image of the destination, and paste it in the circle, or if you want to recover your physical health, look for a picture where you look healthy; if you would like to have a family in union and peace, look for an image that represents that desire. Remember that the picture must be clear and precise, only one per idea, and they are seven ideas.

When you have the seven images pasted on the creation map, hang it in a place where you will see it every day, you can also take a picture of it and put it on your phone screen. The goal is that every day you see the images and have the clarity and accuracy of what you are imagining; many things you want do not materialize because your thinking changes; one day, you want something; another day, something different, and your thinking is an organism of creation. If you choose something and change it, your thought obeys you, and your creation remains dispersed and does not materialize, or it materializes unconsciously, and then you get frustrated. Clarity and accuracy are critical in what you imagine to attract enough materialization energy to create.

Suggestion if you choose to do it freely: look for an image to place on your creation map that signifies reconnection and reactivation with the I AM, or that represents that you are looking for me in your inner self where you rediscover me.

When you have a clear image, the I AM that dwells in you, and you attract the energy from the dimension of the intangible to that of the tangible, and creates reality. Keep firm, clear, and precise in the seven images you have chosen; continuity, focus, clarity, and firmness are a key that open doors to create reality in the physical, mental, and spiritual.

Remember the law of the duality that governs you. If you choose seven ideas based on love for yourself and your fellow man, you will reap good fruits, but if your ego chooses seven ideas based on lovelessness, you will reap poor fruits. Every effect has an initial cause; if you create love, you will receive love, and vice versa. The universal law of duality and cause and effect are mathematical and exact.

Choose to look for me in your inner self at every moment. As you seek me with love, I will guide your thoughts and give you marvelous ideas full of love, and great revelations will come from the innermost part of you.

When there is a union between thought + idea + desire + imagination, we create reality and attract the action that will allow us to have the seven clear ideas we long for in our being and materialize them.

## *5. ACTION*

Action is created when thought, idea, desire, and imagination act coordinated and focused. The sum of these energies creates action, and the universe begins to vibrate at another level attracting the necessary elements to create reality.

The thought generates the action that travels to the intangible dimension, attracts it, and materializes it in the tangible. The action knows the codes to draw materiality.

Every action generates a reaction. **Suggested exercise:** daily, at least once, observe your creation map and read the seven ideas you want to create. As you see and remember the seven ideas you wish to attract from the I AM, it activates in you, generating the action to materialize reality.

The action is to allow things to flow to you naturally; remember that we are using high technology to create a reality with your thought. In the ordinary system of life, we think that action is to go out and, with effort, seek that the seven ideas in the creation map materialize. I tell you that this is not so. Remember that action is fluidity; let things come to you in a natural and balanced way, and if you see that any possible realization of your seven ideas may come with frustration, stress, or fear, discard it. Everything must flow to you in love.

The main action is to experience, know and remember: YOU ARE GOD - YOU ARE GODDESS, I am in you, and I am you...

When there is a union between thought + idea + desire + imagination + action, we create reality and attract the verb that will allow us to have the seven clear ideas of what we long for in our being and materialize them.

## 6. VERB
### John 1:1-3-4

1. In the beginning was the Word, and the Word was with God, and the Word was God.

2. This was at the beginning with God.

3. Through him, all things were made; without him, nothing was made that has been made.

4. And the Word was made flesh, and dwelt among us, and we beheld his glory, the glory as of the only begotten of the Father, full of grace and truth.

**Revelation:**

*1. In the beginning was the Word, and the Word was with God and Goddess, and the Word was God and Goddess.*

*2. This was in the beginning with God and Goddess.*

*3. All things were made by him and her, and without him and her nothing that is made was made.*

*4 And the Word became flesh and dwelt among us, and we saw his glory, glory as of the only begotten of Father and*

*Mother, full of grace and truth.*

Just as I have said to you that YOU ARE GOD - YOU ARE GODDESS, I also say to you:

*YOU ARE THE WORD MADE FLESH...*

When thought, idea, desire, imagination, and action act, the verb (the word) arises. All have been made with the word, and everything that exists and your eyes see has been made by him or her.

What you speak is a consequence of your thought; you must remember how to speak and think consciously so that your fruits are good.

Speech arises from action, and speech manifests matter; a person one-day thought of having some curtains where they live; first, they thought, then an idea arose that attracted a desire, the desire created an image, and from the image arose the action, and from the action arose the verb. Someone's word manifested that he wanted curtains for a window, and the curtains manifested in the dimension of the physical. They were created through the seven steps to create and manifest reality.

**Genesis 1:26 Then God said,** let us make man in our image, after our likeness.

**Revelation: Genesis 1:26 Then God and Goddess said**, *let us make man and woman in our image, after our likeness. (God and Goddess used the word, the verb to create man and woman)*

**Genesis 1:3 And God said,** "Let there be light, and there was light."

**Revelation:** *Genesis 1:3 And God and Goddess said, " Let there be light, and there was light" (God and Goddess used the word, the verb to create)*

*John 1:4* And that Word became flesh and dwelt among us.

Revelation: *John 1:4 And that one and that Word was made and made flesh and dwelt among us. (The word became flesh or you)*

### YOU ARE AND REPRESENT THE WORD MADE FLESH...

When you speak the word, you must remember that the dimension of the intangible and tangible always listens to you and is designed to receive your thoughts whether you do it unconsciously or consciously.

**Practice this exercise:** look at the creation map, now take the first idea and say to the universe: "I AM, I believe here and now", and read affirmatively the seven ideas you have written, whatever you have chosen as the first idea and so on with the others. If more affirmative words arise from within you, let them flow.

If you prefer, write down the decrees on paper to reread them and have them where you are to make the exercise more continuous; remember to affirm with your voice internally and externally.

The verb lives in you. I AM THE VERB: GOD and GODDESS are VERB (Word), YOU ARE VERB, your present is what it is because you have spoken, decreed, and affirmed it unconsciously or consciously. The universe is designed to obey your commands. The more aware you are of me within you, the more your communion with I AM will grow, and the more consciously you will create your reality. Remember to always pay close attention to what you think and speak in your daily life because you can destroy or build; the universe is neutral and obeys you. Enter in communion (Common Union) with I AM in your inner self to discipline your thoughts and words; when you master them, your fruits will change, and you will enter in communion with I God - I Goddess that I AM YOU and YOU ARE ME. You will feel an infinite joy when you reconnect and reactivate yourself.

The sum of these energies creates reality, and the universe begins to vibrate at another level attracting the necessary elements; the word is action and pure movement.

When you create reality, you enter into a spiral of creation where a whole simultaneous process begins and generates a synergy of energies united and intertwined to produce each other: thought + idea + desire + imagination + action + word + gratitude = creation.

All creation is always activated in a circle and triggers the infinite spiral of simultaneous creation synergistically.

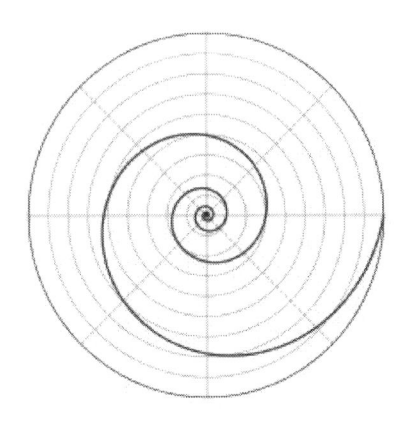

Thought is designed to generate vibrational waves that travel to the intangible world to attract enough matter to the tangible world to create reality. Everything that man builds on a physical, mental, and spiritual level is done by this process.

Any physical object that your eyes see has followed this process, a house, a shirt, a purse, a trip, your health, your abundance, your patience, your humility, your nobility, your love, etc. Before materializing, it was first a thought, an idea, and the whole process that follows is explained here. Think, deepen, reflect, question, analyze this, all before materializing and expressing itself was a thought. When you have this clear in your mind, your being will expand to infinity because you will know how physical, mental, and spiritual matter comes into being.

Likewise, all that happens in your physical, mental, and spiritual body, you created it with your unconscious or conscious thought; that is why I tell you; you are what you think, and what you think, you become at a physical, mental and spiritual level, you are a three-dimensional being that lives an experience in the third dimension which you are experiencing now. If you seek me with determination, persistence, and faith in your inner self, you will find me, and I will guide you and form your conscious thought and character; so be it, and it is.

*Listen to me:* **YOU ARE THE ONE WHO REPRESENTS**

**THE VERB-MADE FLESH...**

**WHEN YOU SPEAK, YOU REPRESENT I AM**

**Exodus 4:12.** "Now go; I will help you speak and will teach you what to say."

**Luke 6:45.** "A good man brings good things out of the good stored up in his heart, and an evil man brings evil things out of the evil stored up in his heart. For the mouth speaks what the heart is full of."

**Ephesians 4:29**. "Do not let any unwholesome talk come out of your mouths, but only what is helpful for building others up according to their needs, that it may benefit those who listen."

**Proverbs 14:4**. "A gentle tongue is a tree of life: but the perverseness thereof is a breaking of the spirit."

Since you are born in this third dimension, you bring the program to create using the verb (the word). Everything exists by the word and all that exists and that your eyes see has been made by him and her; honor your verb with positive words and thus you will honor me.

When there is a union between thought + idea + desire + imagination + action + verb, we create reality and attract the gratitude that will allow us to have the seven clear ideas that we long for in our being and materialize them.

### *7. GRATITUDE*

When thought + idea + desire + imagination + action + verb act, gratitude arises; to give thanks is confirmation and is to have faith that reality will be created. Giving thanks is a spiritual state of supreme knowledge and connection because you know the process of creating reality, and you understand that it is not something mystical or that it happens randomly; you realize that it is a mathematical and exact process that you remember here and now. Everything in the universe has a cause and an effect. All happen mathematically and have an explanation. My creation is based on science, that is, cause and effect. What you call miracles, has a cause and effect; often, your society cannot find or understand the first cause. Just because there is no explanation does not mean there is no first cause.

Gratitude activates the I AM in the process of creation. You give thanks because these seven ideas that we are creating already are. You thank God - Goddess within you because we brought these seven realities into being.

When you thank me, you activate the union between YOU and me, and we become one. The universe is full of gratitude, which is love flowing and creating. Gratitude is a state of being that understands that all already is and happens.

When you give thanks before a reality materializes, you attract what you desire. Gratitude activates the verb powerfully, raises the energy and attracts reality and materialization.

I suggest you create your seven ideas as a game as if you were a child. Play with the program to create reality. Remember that when you were a child and played, your imagination flew through infinity. You did not care about the result; you had fun playing; you were happy and lived in the present. Remember when you rode a bike or ran freely, without the desire to arrive; you just pedaled or moved, and you liked to feel the air on your face and the feeling of freedom. I invite you to make this process of creating these seven ideas like a game, a fun creation game, play with this, have fun, think that you are playing and creating, and free yourself from pressuring the result. When you push the result to materialize, anxiety and fear quickly arise. I know you are an adult, and maybe you forgot to play; now, it is time to remember and play again.

**Matthew 18:3.** "And he said: Truly I tell you, unless you change and become like little children, you will never enter the kingdom of heaven."

Possibly in this creation process, you feel anxiety and desperation to achieve quick results; maybe you wonder how much the seven ideas will materialize and materialize. I tell you: be patient when creating because you have moved away from me, and you are entering a new cycle of reconnection and reactivation. As long as you remain firm with will, concentration, courage, perseverance, and faith, the fruits will come to you, do it with a noble and free heart. In this process, possibly your ego and desires, negative energies want to try to manipulate the universe to get immediate or fanciful results; I tell you: be patient in the process. To create reality at will, if you do it with a noble heart and freely, gradually, you will remember and reactivate the process.

In higher dimensions, where beings are more conscious of the I AM within themselves, they instantly create reality at will. The third dimension in which you dwell is denser, and the processes become slower, stand firm with courage, will, faith, determination, concentration, enthusiasm, and persistence with the seven ideas, and the fruits will come to you. The process of creating reality is like when you plant a tree to have good fruits. First, you get the seed, then you open a hole in the ground, sow the seed, put water and fertilizer, watch the stem grow, put more water, then the leaves grow, and finally, harvest the fruits, but the harvest is not immediate. I tell you that the speed of creation increases when you are more conscious and you find me in your inner self.

In this moment of unconsciousness and simultaneous consciousness in which you are, you create by trial and error.

Your creations are so because you have lost the knowledge that I dwell in you and YOU and I AM ONE. The beauty, perfection, and beauty of this reconnection and reactivation that is coming to you now are that you attracted it, and we are on the right track...

**Reflect, deepen, analyze, question, and think about the following:**

Everything that exists and has a physical, mental, and spiritual manifestation follows the mathematical and exact order of how reality is created: thought + idea + desire + imagination + imagination + action + verb + gratitude = creation.

The now offers you infinite opportunities, and there will always be something to choose and recreate. You create your present. All can be transformed. The universe is as flexible as your thoughts. Nothing is rigidly written. There are infinite possibilities here and now, and the one you choose and create will materialize. You and your society can choose among endless choices in the here and now and also towards what you call the future. Every prophecy can be transformed and transmuted. If a great mass of human beings has a common thought, they can change the destiny of humanity. Unity is strength and creates reality.

Through the seven steps to creating reality, all have been created. The system brings into being simple and small things but also big and majestic ones that your thinking can imagine. Remember: I AM the micro and the macro, and I dwell in the visible and invisible. Unite in loving thought, you and your fellows, and thus you will be able to transform the world and bring it to love, freedom, and truth. So be it, and it is.

## Universal Law of Duality

It is essential that you deepen, reflect, analyze, and think about the universal laws that are given to you in this message because as you remember them, your level of consciousness will grow; you will understand in depth how the third dimension works in which you inhabit in body, mind, and spirit.

When you incarnate in the third dimension and enter through the door of duality, you forget a part of your connection to divinity and other realities of being in higher dimensions. Remember: You have freely chosen to come here, to live and experience duality. In the universe, all is free will.

When you pass through the doorway of the third dimension, you enter duality, and that law will govern you as long as you are incarnated. Through this message, I will remind you of what this universal law is composed of so that you can identify, know and transmute it.

Duality is the principle of what is not and what is, what you know as evil and good, darkness and light, separation and union, irrational and rational, sickness and health, scarcity and abundance, fear and love.

Everything you create and experience in the eternal present on the physical, mental, and spiritual levels is governed by the universal law of duality. Your thoughts are vibrating in negative or positive energy. The balance is charged with these energies. Every action you take rules a negative or positive energy. I Goddess - I God, who dwells in you, am always positive energy.

When your thinking is charged with positive energy, you attract positive energies that will attract other positive forces that will lead you to reap abundant and good fruits physically, mentally, and spiritually. Your harvest will be according to what you sow; if your thinking gets charged with negative energies, you will attract negative forces that will attract other negative energies that will lead you to harvest scarce and poor fruits at the physical, mental, and spiritual levels.

Duality governs the human being physically, mentally, and spiritually. Whatever you concentrate your thoughts on, fear or love, you will attract reality in fear or love. You must pay close attention to what you think and speak, always moving towards love, light, union, rationality, sincerity, honesty, etc. Remember that to think is to create. When you experience positive energies of love, peace, happiness, fullness, tranquility, etc., in your being, you are in union with I God - I Goddess who dwells in you. When you experience negative energies, you are separated from me.

The system society where you dwell now constantly attacks you with negative energies by all means and systems; they instill fear incessantly. I tell you that they want to take you away from me and make you believe that you are in fear and darkness. Even though your essence and lineage are love, if you transmit fear, you will be controlled and enslaved, and through that strategy of fear, you will be separated from I God - I Goddess, who am you and live within you.

You must concentrate on positive energies such as love and those that emanate from it, such as union, peace, relaxation, kindness, compassion, honesty, tranquility, solace, fraternity, abundance, etc. When you vibrate with these energies, it is a sign that we are united.

I tell you: from now on when your thoughts and actions are

charged with negative energies, think:

What would love to do?

How would love act?

I WILL ENLIGHTEN YOU AND TELL YOU WHAT LOVE WOULD DO... AND I WILL TELL YOU HOW LOVE WOULD ACT...

Seek me with a noble heart within, and I will guide you and remind you how to identify and attract positive energies into your life.

### How to transmute duality?

Start by thinking and acting in love towards yourself and your fellow men. When you concentrate your thoughts and energy on positive energies, your results and being will rise positively.

### What is transmutation?

Transmutation is what is known as alchemy, which is the conversion of a lower negative energy into a higher positive energy.

What you call sin or virtue is duality. In the dimension where I live, duality is an illusion that does not exist; you have negative and positive energies; concentrate on the positive ones. *I invite you to do the following exercise:* make a list of the positive energies that you consider you have, write them down so you can affirm them, and hold on to them. You will attract more good vibrations as you affirm them and engrave them in your being. Each positive energy is a living spiritual-energetic being; when you are calm or happy, an energetic being is with you. When there are positive energies in your thought, such as love, charity, temperance, humility, nobility, sincerity, abundance, etc., each of these energies is a living spiritual being that accompanies you and joins you because you attract it with your thought and creative desire. Remember that it also works the other way around.

When you unite with positive energies, you attract other positive energies and radiate them to your fellow men and women; you become a propagator of love, tranquility, peace, charity, humility, abundance, nobility, happiness, patience, etc. Remember that every moment you inhale and exhale, you receive and emit energy; you are a constant transmitter of negative or positive energy. If you choose to grow spiritually, every moment you reconnect and reactivate with the I AM, you will remember and vibrate higher, thus emitting more positive energies, or light, to your fellow man. At the moment of reconnection with the I God - I Goddess within you, there will be times when negative energies will seek to divert and de-concentrate you from your choice of spiritual growth; when this happens, seek me within you, ask for my guidance and I will come to you and remind you how to transmute those negative energies. Remember and reflect on this: What you focus on will expand, and that is what you will attract.

Constantly watch how you feed your physical body, mind, and spirit; as you remember how to do this, you will attract more positive energies. The world you live in is full of negative energies in food, music, the internet, tv, radio, cinema, media, education, artificial intelligence, algorithms, metaverse, holography, virtual reality, etc. Likewise, your world is also full of positive energies. This message comes to you because your society tends to tip the balance to the side of negative energies. It is vitally important that your society realizes that this is happening, and when they do, they can transmute it and move the balance to the side of positive energies.

Positive energies on the spiritual, mental, and physical planes feed on positive energies and vice versa. You must be aware that you nourish with your thoughts, emotions, and feelings, beings of positive energy or beings of negative energy. Your thoughts, emotions, and feelings are vibrations and energy; depending on where you vibrate, you will be nurturing negative or positive energy beings.

All negative energy is an attachment that we cling to; that negative energy will disappear when you transcend it and transmute it with positive energy. The principle to transmute a negative energy is to identify it. For example, when you recognize, analyze, reflect, and observe that you have anxiety in your life, you have the possibility that the I from within you transmute it into tranquility. When some negative energy comes to your thoughts, **perform this exercise:**

Suppose you feel anxiety. First, think and identify this negative energy. After realizing that you have it, think of me, invoke me from your thought, and say: God - Goddess that dwells in me, guide me to transmute this negative energy of anxiety, do it with faith, and I will come to you, and guide you to transmute it. Test me in this, and I will come to you with light, vibration, and wisdom.

It is healthy to accept that you have negative energies; that is the first step to transmute them. When you identify it, you can transmute that negative energy into positive for your spiritual growth. For example, if you are grumpy and realize and accept it from your heart, you can transmute it. When you identify negative energy with your thinking, the possibility arises to transmute it and create positive energy.

Duality is like a mirror where you can see your negative and positive sides; it allows you to live with enlightened and dark aspects. The universal law of duality governs every moment of all human beings regardless of their beliefs, opinions, studies, or tenancies.

Every human being plays a role in the harmony and perfection of the planet. Every positive or negative thought and feeling affect humanity; every time you think, your thoughts influence others.

Respect and love others for what they are, not who you want them to be, so you can transcend the judgment of duality. Stop judging, and the pain will disappear. I AM does not judge or condemn.

Duality is disconnection and forgetfulness. Duality is believing that you are separate from me. It is not about judging what is wrong or correct; it is about identifying negative energies, recognizing them, observing them, and analyzing them to transmute them. When you identify a negative energy, you will transmute it if you come to me internally. I will guide you on how to do it.

The purpose of the negative energies is to separate you from the I Goddess - I God who dwells within you. As you get more separated from me, you will be more vulnerable to being controlled and enslaved by those negative energies; that is what the duality game you freely chose to experience here is all about. Duality is possible in the third dimension. In higher dimensions, duality is fictitious and unreal; it does not exist. In higher dimensions, the only real thing is love.

Every time you inhale and exhale, your body, mind, and spirit are fed with negative or positive energies. It is crucial to remember how to nourish and attract positive energies; when you remember this, your vital energy and vibration rise and attract more positive energies; when you imbibe and unite with these energies, you are surrounded by even more positive vibrational energies. Remember that each positive or negative energy is a being that exists and has life; you give them life through your thoughts, emotions, actions, words, and feelings. When you attract positive energies, you will also be a transmitter of them and vice versa. Also, when you charge yourself with negative energies, every moment you inhale or exhale, you transmit negative or positive energies. It is important to remember how to tip the balance towards the positive side. When you reconnect with I AM and enter a higher level of vibrational communion, you attract positive energies into your life, family, and world. When you raise your vibration and frequency by creating positive energies, you will change the world; as more beings practice and rediscover this, your world will grow towards harmony and perfection.

Look at the negative energy of anxiety or any other because by experiencing anxiety and then transmuting it into tranquility, you will value and understand tranquility in depth. See duality as an experience to reach love and reconnection with I AM. Experiencing duality is essential to healing and creating balance.

The purpose and objective of negative energies are to keep you unconscious of the I AM within. When this happens, you will be tainted with negative energies in your physical, mental, and spiritual body, and you will be vulnerable to being controlled, enslaved, and separated from the I AM within you.

When you remember and transcend that duality is an illusion and that it is becoming easier to attract positive energies and beings into your life, it will be a sign that you are reconnecting with I AM and entering into another level of communion with I Goddess - I God who dwells within you. You are my temple, and I abide in you.

**How Can I Recognize and Know That It Is Your Voice?**

I will always speak to you from love and light. You will be inspired to act with joy and love, so you can know that it IS ME talking to you from within.

*All negative energy is contagious and is a virus that deprograms and uniforms you; all positive energy is duplicable and programs and informs you, generating benefits at the level of your physical, mental, and spiritual body.*

Any negative energy inserted into you by different means, such as TV, radio, internet, artificial intelligence, algorithms, holography, cinema, metaverse, virtual reality, etc., are viruses that disinform and deprogram you. When this happens, the communion with I AM is distorted, and your reconnection and reactivation with I Goddess - I God becomes diminished.

The lies that many times you are inoculated by the different communication systems that you read, hear or see are misinformative viruses, living energies that deprogram you. The more you receive disinformation, the more you will be deprogrammed and the more difficult it will become for you to enter into reconnection and communion with I God - I Goddess.

Any negative energy that society inserts in you through what you read, hear, or see is a virus that disinforms and deprograms you. Seek me within, and I will guide you to recognize the truth from the lie. Ask me, and I will answer you. You are worthy to communicate with I AM, even if your mind and reasoning tell you that you are not. Seek me, and you will find me. In this message, I give you several tools that will allow you to deepen and know the eternal union between YOU and ME.

Duality, or what your society calls evil and good, is part of my divine plan to experience myself through you and raise my universal consciousness about how I create and re-create myself infinitely. To transcend and transmute duality, seek to unify with I Goddess - I God within you, and when you find me, you will awaken from your deep sleep transcending the fiction and fantasy of the ego.

# The Balance of Evil and Good

| Negative Energies | Positive Energies |
|---|---|
| The Evil | The Good |
| Darkness | Light |
| Hate | Love |
| Separation | Union |
| Deprogramming | Programming |
| Unconsciousness | Conscience |
| Disinformation | Information |
| Ignorance | Knowledge |
| Disharmony | Harmony |
| Imperfection | Perfection |
| Dissatisfaction | Satisfaction |
| Degeneration | Generation |
| Incomprehension | Compression |
| Abnormality | Normality |
| Sadness | Happiness |
| Shortage | Abundance |
| Lie | Truth |
| Illness | Health |
| Imbalance | Equilibrium |
| Malnutrition | Nutrition |
| Disorder | Order |
| Roughness | Delicacy |
| Violence | Peace |
| Ugliness | Beauty |
| Destruction | Construction |
| Slavery | Freedom |
| Pride | Humility |
| Unnatural | Natural |
| Hypocrisy | Sincerity |
| Impatience | Patience |
| Disrespect | Respect |
| Distrust | Trust |
| Noise | Sound |
| Attachment | Detachment |
| Irrational | Rational |
| Vice | Habit |
| Distortion | Vibration |
| Inculturation | Culture |
| Disrespect | Respect |
| Emptiness | Fullness |
| Dishonesty | Honesty |
| Pessimism | Optimism |

Remember that a negative energy, mathematically and scientifically, can never generate a positive one, and a positive energy can never degenerate into a negative one. Hate can never generate love, separation can never generate union, hate will always degenerate and attract other similar energies such as lack of love, frustration, anger, etc., and love will always originate and attract similar energies such as relaxation, fulfillment, happiness, union, etc.

I say to you: a positive energy contains all positive energies simultaneously and multi-dimensionally, and a negative energy contains all negative energies simultaneously and multi-dimensionally.

Remember that my most powerful messenger is experience. The more you experience, test, think, question, ponder, reflect, practice this book's message, the more you will know, and the more you remember who you are, the more you will desire to experience your divine lineage and lineage. Remember that you can only live what you know.

## Universal Law of Cause and Effect

Everything physical, mental, and spiritual has a cause and an effect; what you experience today had an initial cause generated by you; nothing happens randomly or by chance in the universe. What you are today, you created it with your thoughts. I do not give or take anything away from you; you create it unconsciously or consciously through the software called thought. Religiosity has made you believe that I give you or take away according to your conduct or that the more you beg, sacrifice, and pray, the more I give you. I tell you that this is incongruent, illogical, and fanciful when you are indoctrinated that I God - I Goddess give or take away is a dogma used to distract you, deceive you, enslave you, and control you. They have indoctrinated you to make you dependent on a manipulative religious system; religions have existed for thousands of years because they indoctrinated you to give them your power. I tell you: you will get what you create with your thoughts; it is time for you to look for me within yourself, reconnect, reactivate, and enter into communion (common union) and lead humanity to a new awakening, where each being will rediscover God-Goddess within, and create a new stage of reunion and reconnection with the God-Goddess that dwells in you, and your fellow men.

All the time, you are sowing initial causes, and all begins with a thought. You must always be vigilant about what you think because all you call reality is first born in your thinking. Say what you think, and I will tell you who you are; tell me what you think, and I will tell you what you believe. Always remember the universal law of cause and effect that governs you; what you sow, in your thought, you will reap.

The universal law of cause and effect is governed by the

physical, mental, and spiritual. If you educate a child with positive energies, that child will be a citizen who will contribute to the benefit of society. If you educate a child with negative energies, such as listening to obscene lyrics and melodies loaded with noise, that child will become a problem for his parents and society. What you sow, you will reap; if the world makes wars and invests in weapons, it will reap famine, desolation, and chaos. Everything is mathematical, cause and effect; nothing happens at random. This law governs all areas of society, so from now on, you should focus on knowing what causes you sow because mathematically you will reap what you sow. You can change your reality if you change your thoughts and concentrate on having thoughts based on love, charity, kindness, altruism, abundance, etc. As you master your thoughts with positive energies, you will reap good fruits. Come to me in your inner self, invoke my guidance, and I will guide you.

The universal law of cause and effect governs all the arts, engineering, physics, chemistry, mathematics, architecture, psychology, medicine, philosophy, spirituality, science, religions, politics, media, society, love, abundance, honesty, sincerity, philosophy, truth, etc. Delve into this law that will bring many revelations into your life and allow you to see many deceptions to which you are subjected daily through TV, radio, internet, artificial intelligence, algorithms, metaverse, holography, virtual reality, etc. You are constantly induced with fear so that you absorb it, and your thoughts are based on fear, and your fruits are unhealthy. Seek me within with a pure heart, and I will remind you how to create thought causes based on love and abundance.

The system society in which you live induces and indoctrinates you to think wrongly, to believe and recreate always the same negative energies. You are flooded with fear, and if there is fear in your heart, your thinking is clouded, and you will create more fear. When you think with fear, you finish creating more fear, which is what you are not. The real virus inserted at every moment you inhale and exhale is the virus of fear, which is inoculated by different media such as TV, radio, the internet, cinema, artificial intelligence, metaverse algorithms, holography, virtual reality, etc. By spreading the virus of fear, you get infected and infect your fellow men; fear is the real pandemic of which you are constantly and aggressively infected. Through constant fear, you contaminate yourself and your fellow men. The more fear you have, the more negative energies you will attract, and thus you will unconsciously infect your fellow men, the virus of fear is destroying your society and allowing you to disconnect yourself from the I God - I Goddess that dwells in you. When you are afraid, you separate yourself and doubt ME; this message comes to you to remember and reactivate how to transmit love in you and your fellow men. Here you will find the keys that open the doors that will allow you to be one with I AM and attract positive energies to the world.

You are the only one responsible for what you are living today. I understand that you think I created this reality or situation that distresses you for so long. I am telling you that at some point, you sowed an initial cause in your thinking unconsciously or consciously; that is why you manifested that reality. Now you know how to reverse the process, and it is by recreating a different initial cause in your thinking so that your fruit will be healthy. Those who look for me in the heavens or fantasy and unreachable places do it because they want to depend on something unreal that not even their religions can explain. If you want to grow and evolve physically, mentally, and spiritually, an important step is to accept that you created your reality; be responsible, and to the extent that you understand your responsibility, you will transmute it. You were created in the image and likeness of I AM, and you create your reality through your unconscious or conscious thought. You have inherited my creative essence, and that truly lives and is present at every moment of the now in your physical, mental, and spiritual body.

Religiosity has led you to beg God for things, and with this false dogma, millions of people ask God to give them health, abundance, material things, etc. Millions of people spend their whole life asking God for something, and they say: "Oh" what an incomprehensible God that gives to some and not to others, what a Machiavellian God that gives to some quickly, and others die, and they never get what they ask for. I tell you: you will get what you believe with your unconscious or conscious thought. The responsibility for what you are currently experiencing is yours; to the extent that you become aware of that responsibility, you can change the situation. In this message that comes to your hands are the tools if you choose to change using your free will.

I God - I Goddess am science, cause, and effect, I AM, and I vibrate in this universal law, take out of your mind that I am a mystical, fantastic, inexplicable, incomprehensible, unreachable God or that I am in a distant and inaccessible place or the way you imagined me on the outside. Listen to me, and look for me in your inner self with a noble heart, and you will find me, observe the course of a river and its natural, orderly, and balanced movement; it is perfect. Observe your life; it moves like your heart, in complete harmony and synchrony; it palpitates and vibrates to give you life every day; all have a logical and exact order in my creation. By deepening, reflecting, questioning, and thinking about the law of cause and effect, you will be able to know me deeply, and doors of pure knowledge will open for you.

The unfavorable effects that humanity reaps today are because they are separated from the knowledge of the universal law of cause and effect. If you sow a good seed, you will reap good fruits; this law governs you and your fellow men. What you sow, you will reap; what your society sows, they will reap mathematically and infallibly. From now on, every time you have a thought and later an idea, go deep into it; if that idea is based on love, it comes from me. If an idea comes to you based on lovelessness, envy, fear, lies, anger, etc., seek me within and speak to me, I AM will hear you. Bring me your pure thoughts, and I AM will guide you so you can transmute your thoughts into positive energies. I GOD - I GODDESS am always for you within you; remember that the natural law of cause and effect governs you every moment of your life, and every initial cause that you sow is based on two emotions which are fear and love. Choose love as your initial cause, and your fruits will bless you physically, mentally, and spiritually.

As you find me in your inner self by your own choice and free will, I will guide you to focus your thoughts properly, sowing causes based on love, abundance, union, happiness, peace, balance, etc. Just as you have erroneous causes that you have planted by unconsciousness, I will guide you so that you can transmute negative energies and sow positive energies to achieve pleasant and healthy effects. Remember that all the power of the universe lies within you, and it is infinitely possible to transmute any energy or reality created. The universe and reality are as flexible as your thought. Your thought is designed to influence and transform matter and is as infinitely pliable as you create it.

The positive effects you have in your life are because you think rightly, and the adverse effects are because you think wrongly. By thinking with positive energy, you can also heal; diseases, in a large percentage, are born from not knowing the effects of sowing incorrect physical, mental, and spiritual nutrition. Your purest medicine to heal you is within you. I can heal you if you look for me and imagine me in your inner self. When you remember and master the universal law of cause and effect, you can reverse your physical, mental, and spiritual problems.

Societies more advanced than yours understand in depth the universal law of cause and effect; they practice and know it, and they are societies that transmit this wisdom to all their generations. Having clarity and awareness of this law allows them to advance to other states of knowledge and spirituality because they become aware of their responsibility, what they create, and what governs them to evolve and rise to higher levels of communion with I AM. Remember that I am also within them.

The most divine, magnificent, beautiful, and wonderful being you can imagine is in you.

The same essence of mine that lies and dwells in Jesus, Buddha, Krishna, the virgin, saints, teachers, angels, archangels, gurus, coaches, priests, shepherds, extraterrestrials, etc., all these beings that you admire, respect, follow and pay obeisance to are in you in the same quantity and substance. I tell you: ***the same essence of mine in them is in you; the difference between them and you is their more advanced level of I AM consciousness within you.***

I say to you: no matter your mistakes or successes, stay away from the inserted dogma of guilt or that you feel unworthy or undeserving. I dwell in you, and I AM LOVE; love does not judge; it only loves.

Religions instilled guilt into you to keep your consciousness trapped in pain and distort your true self. You transmute the above by communing and reconnecting with the I AM within you.

When you sow a cause of love, you receive an effect of love and vice versa; it is like that mathematically, cause and effect. What you do has a consequence; you are responsible for the initial causes, you sow with your thoughts, every action has a reaction, all energy generates waves and effects, everything you give, you receive, and what others experience for you, you will experiment later.

If you sow lies, you will attract lies; if you judge, you will be judged; if you sow love, you will reap love; if you sow kindness, you will reap kindness, no more, no less; it is mathematical, cause and effect is a boomerang, what comes out of you comes back to you. If your initial causes are healthy, your fruits will be beneficial. The universal laws are exact and mathematical; you are free, sovereign, and responsible for your actions. You created your current situation and what you are, unconsciously or consciously; nothing in the universe happens randomly; everything has a cause and an effect; it is mathematical. Reflect, think, question, and analyze this.

If you look for me in your inner self to give you physical, mental, or spiritual things, you will not find me. If you look for me in your inner self with a noble heart to guide you and reactivate in you the knowledge and wisdom on how to create with positive energy your physical, mental, and spiritual reality, you will find me.

When you become more aware that every cause has an effect and that depending on the cause you build, so will your fruits, you will evolve to another level of knowledge and understanding where your fruits will be clean and pure. Choose freely to be aware and deepen that every cause has an effect that governs you here and now in your physical, mental, and spiritual development. I insist, in the universe, nothing happens randomly or by causality; everything is mathematical and synchronized regardless of your unconsciousness or consciousness. This message comes to you to reprogram you and to remember who you are; YOU ARE GODDESS - YOU ARE GOD.

I AM A GOD AND GODDESS OF LOVE, but remember that every moment, you are governed by the universal law of cause and effect; no one on the face of the earth can deceive or circumvent this law. What you sow, you will reap unfailingly.

The door of responsibility is opened, and few brave people dare to accept it. They usually leave the commitment to the fanciful God, who is in the heavens or far away and unreachable, because apparently, it is easier to leave the responsibility to chance, to the imaginary and the mystical. Perhaps, it is easier to delegate your power and truth to others' hands. You do it because you still believe you are separate from the I AM, or you can continue to believe in false and fanciful dogmas because you lack the courage and bravery to accept your responsibility.

*The true and pure warrior of light is the one who takes responsibility for themselves and their creations.*

# Sacred Words and Decrees to Create Reality in Your Daily Life

## *Seven Keys to Create Reality at Will*

### John 1:1-3-4

1. In the beginning was the Word, and the Word was with God, and the Word was God.

2. He was with God in the beginning.

3. Through him, all things were made; without him, nothing was made that has been made.

4 And the Word was made flesh and dwelt among us, and we saw his glory; the glory as of the only begotten of the Father, full of grace and truth.

### Revelation:

*1. In the beginning was the Word, and the Word was with God and Goddess, and the Word was God and Goddess.*

*2. He was with God and Goddess in the beginning.*

*3. Through him and her, all things were made; without him and her, nothing was made that has been made.*

*4. And the Word became flesh and dwelt among us, and we saw his glory, the glory as of the only begotten of Father and Mother, full of grace and truth.*

When you affirm, decree, and practice the conscious verb of I, you reconnect and reactivate with the I AM within you, and there arises within you your Creator God and your Creator Goddess who lives and lies within you.

In this message, you will remember seven powerful decrees to create and transform through the verb (The Word) your present reality.

Everything you live and experience today in what you call life, you created through your thought, word, and deed. When you remember this sacred knowledge, you will change your reality. Nothing comes to you by chance; all you have brought to your life is through your conscious or unconscious thought. You create your reality, and in every moment, you forge your eternal present with your thoughts and choices. Religions misinform you and make you believe that the fruits of your life are by chance or some other mystical or mysterious circumstance that only the most learned or chosen can understand. I say to you: free yourself and be responsible for what you create with your thinking.

Society indoctrinates you to make you believe that there is not, that I do not have, that I cannot, that I am not, that I do not do, that I do not know, that I do not give. Through the continuous implantation of these thoughts, you are enslaved and frightened day by day in different ways, through TV, the internet, education, media, governments, cinema, religions, artificial intelligence, algorithms, metaverse, holograms, etc.

This message comes to you by causality; you have created it yourself. Now I give you seven keys that will make your union with I AM in your inner self more solid and real at every instant of the eternal present. Engrave these seven keys in you because they open the door to multiple dimensions, record them, remember them, share them, and practice them in each inhale and exhale of your eternal present.

## 1. KEY: I HAVE

## What do you have if you were created in the image and likeness of God and Goddess?

When a thinking arises in you about something you want to improve, overcome, transmute, or recreate, again say in your thought and with your words I HAVE health, I HAVE abundance, I HAVE love for me and to give, I HAVE wisdom, etc. Always saying and thinking I HAVE. When you use the I decree, you unite with I AM, and conscious creation arises. The universe is a perfect organism and is at your service, it was conceived and designed to obey you. Remember that in everything that happens in your life, you created it consciously or unconsciously; the universe responds to you, whether your thoughts are charged with negative or positive energies. This message is for you to remember and reprogram your life freely if you choose to do so.

When you think and say, I would like to have health, I would like to have abundance, the universe obeys you, but "I would like" is someday, maybe tomorrow or in 30 years. The decree I would like is ephemeral and can be at any moment, but when you say I HAVE, the energetic vibration of the command is to create that reality right now, in the eternal present. Remember, from now on, to practice I HAVE; when you do, you will experience that your creations crystallize quickly, and thus the level of reality will manifest easier in the third dimension.

You must be attentive when you say I DO NOT HAVE this or that because you manifest that decree and the universe obeys you, it creates that reality for you. The universe is designed to be neutral and follow what you build, whether negative or positive. For this reason, you must pay close attention to what you speak because the universe is ready to listen and execute your desires and attract that reality into your life. Words have power and create reality; remember that in the beginning was the word, and the word was with God and Goddess, and the word was God and Goddess, and they have created your present reality. The word that comes out of your being is sacred to the universe.

When the current society tells you, in many ways and by different means, that you do not have, that there is scarcity or there is not enough of this or that, **do this exercise:** breathe deeply and slowly seven times, and imagine that I GOD - I GODDESS am within you and I tell you yes there is, yes you have, yes, there is enough, YES, I HAVE. Mathematically and infallibly, the universe is created on the laws of YES, I HAVE. With your thought, you bring this reality into being. Free yourself from the yoke of the slave society, and remember to assert your freedom, sovereignty, and lineage. YOU ARE GODDESS - YOU ARE GOD, and create every moment your reality.

When you use the word, say with your physical, mental, and spiritual body, I HAVE; by speaking it, you are affirming and attracting the energies and vibrations to create that reality in your life. Remember that positive energy attracts to you, through your thoughts, other beings with positive vibrations and vice versa.

What you affirm is created, and that is what you become; tell me what you speak, and I will tell you who you are.

Remember: everything in the universe works by merit, development, willpower, and surrender. The most evolved beings in the universe have been able to rise and unite to higher levels with I AM within because they have freely chosen to do so through their love, persistence, concentration, practice, courage, process, and merit. Remember that deservedness is built through the positive energies you sow in yourself and your fellow man. Remove from your mind the false dogma that I choose a privileged few and not others. I tell you: I AM LOVE, and all are included and selected in our kingdom.

When you use and practice the I HAVE affirmatively, you honor me.

Whenever a desire arises about something you want to transmute, improve or obtain on a physical, mental, and spiritual level, think and say: **I HAVE**. As you practice it, this key will open the doors to new knowledge, and you will be practicing and deserving to raise the level of union with I GOD - I GODDESS that dwells in you, and I AM YOU, YOU ARE GODDESS - YOU ARE GOD.

I honor you from eternity, and I AM I, for YOU and I ONE ARE; your presence in me is deserved forever and ever; So be it, and it is.

### 2. KEY: I CAN

### What can you do if you were created in the image and likeness of God and Goddess?

When a thought arises in you about something you want to improve, overcome, transmute, or recreate, say in your mind and with your words, I CAN be happy, I CAN be kind, I CAN give love, I CAN be abundant, I CAN be healthy, I CAN be spiritual, etc. Always use the I CAN when you make the decree. The I unites with the I AM, and conscious creation arises. The universe is a perfect organism and is at your service; it was conceived and designed to obey you. Remember that everything that happens in your life, you created consciously or unconsciously; the universe responds to you regardless of whether your thoughts are negative or positive. This message is for you to remember and reprogram your life freely if you choose to do so.

When you think and say, if I could have health, or If I could have abundance, the universe obeys you, but "If I could" is someday, maybe tomorrow or in 30 years. The decree "if I could" is ephemeral and can be at any moment, but when you say I CAN, the energetic vibration of the command is to create that reality right now, in the eternal present. Remember, from now on, to practice the I CAN; when you do, you will experience that your creations crystallize quickly, and thus the level of reality will manifest easier in the third dimension.

You must be attentive when you say I CANNOT this or that because you manifest that decree, and the universe obeys you; it creates that reality for you. The universe is designed to be neutral and follow what you build, whether negative or positive. For this reason, you must pay close attention to what you speak because the universe is ready to listen and execute your desires and attract that reality into your life. Words have power and create reality; remember that in the beginning was the word, and the word was with God and Goddess, and the word was God and Goddess, and they have created your present reality. The word that comes out of your being is sacred to the universe.

When the current society tells you, in many ways and by different means, that you do not have, that there is scarcity or there is not enough of this or that, **do this exercise:** breathe deeply and slowly seven times, and imagine that I GOD - I GODDESS am within you and I tell you yes you are capable, yes you can, yes, it is possible, YES, I CAN. Mathematically and infallibly, the universe is created on the laws of YES, I CAN. With your thought, you bring this reality into being. Free yourself from the yoke of the slave society, and remember to assert your freedom, sovereignty, and lineage. YOU ARE GODDESS - YOU ARE GOD, and create every moment your reality.

When you use the word, say with your physical, mental, and spiritual body, I CAN; by speaking it, you are affirming and attracting the energies and vibrations to create that reality in your life. Remember that positive energy attracts to you, through your thoughts, other beings with positive vibrations and vice versa.

What you affirm is created, and that is what you become; tell me what you speak, and I will tell you who you are.

Remember: everything in the universe works by merit, development, willpower, and surrender. The most evolved beings in the universe have been able to rise and unite to higher levels with I AM within because they have freely chosen to do so through their love, persistence, concentration, practice, courage, process, and merit. Remember that deservedness is built through the positive energies you sow in yourself and your fellow man. Remove from your mind the false dogma that I choose a privileged few and not others. I tell you: I AM LOVE, and all are included and selected in our kingdom.

When you use and practice the I CAN affirmatively, honor me.

Whenever a desire arises about something you want to transmute, improve or obtain on a physical, mental and spiritual level, think and say: **I CAN**. As you practice it, this key will open the doors to new knowledge, and you will be practicing and deserving to raise the level of union with I GOD - I GODDESS that dwells in you, and I AM YOU, YOU ARE GODDESS - YOU ARE GOD.

I honor you from eternity, and I AM I, for YOU and I ONE ARE; your presence in me is deserved forever and ever; So be it, and it is.

### 3. KEY: I KNOW

### What do you know if you were created in the image and likeness of God and Goddess?

When a thought is born in you about something you want to improve, overcome, transmute, or recreate, say in your mind and with your words, I KNOW how to be happy, I KNOW how to be kind, I KNOW how to give love, I KNOW how to be healthy, I KNOW how to feed myself correctly, I KNOW how to be abundant, I KNOW how to be healthy, I KNOW how to be spiritual, etc. Always using the I KNOW when you make the decree. The universe is a perfect organism and is at your service; it was conceived and designed to obey you. Remember that everything that happens in your life, you created consciously or unconsciously; the universe responds to you regardless of whether your thoughts are negative or positive. This message is for you to remember and reprogram your life freely if you choose to do so.

When you think and say, I don't know, the universe obeys you and creates that reality for you; the universe is at your service and obeys you. But when you say I KNOW the energetic vibration of the decree is to create that reality right now in the eternal present. Remember from now on to practice the I KNOW; when you do, you will begin to see that your creations will crystallize quickly, and thus the level of reality will manifest easier in the third dimension.

You must be attentive when you say I DON'T KNOW this or that because you manifest that decree, and the universe obeys you; it creates that reality for you. The universe is designed to be neutral and follow what you build, whether negative or positive. For this reason, you must pay close attention to what you speak because the universe is ready to listen and execute your desires and attract that reality into your life. Words have power and create reality; remember that in the beginning was the word, and the word was with God and Goddess, and the word was God and Goddess, and they have created your present reality. The word that comes out of your being is sacred to the universe.

When the current society tells you in many ways and by different means that you do not know or that only they know, **do this exercise:** breathe deeply and slowly seven times and imagine that I GOD - I GODDESS am in your inner self, and I tell you YES YOU KNOW. Mathematically and infallibly, the universe is created on the laws of YES, I KNOW. With your thought, you bring this reality into being. Free yourself from the yoke of the slave society, and remember to assert your freedom, sovereignty, and lineage. YOU ARE GODDESS - YOU ARE GOD, and create every moment your reality.

When you use the word, say with your physical, mental, and

spiritual body, I KNOW; by speaking it, you are affirming and attracting the energies and vibrations to create that reality in your life. Remember that positive energy attracts to you, through your thoughts, other beings with positive vibrations and vice versa.

What you affirm is created, and that is what you become; tell me what you speak, and I will tell you who you are.

Remember: everything in the universe works by merit, development, willpower, and surrender. The most evolved beings in the universe have been able to rise and unite to higher levels with I AM within because they have freely chosen to do so through their love, persistence, concentration, practice, courage, process, and merit. Remember that deservedness is built through the positive energies you sow in yourself and your fellow man. Remove from your mind the false dogma that I choose a privileged few and not others. I tell you: I AM LOVE, and all are included and selected in our kingdom.

When you use and practice the I KNOW affirmatively, you honor me.

Whenever a desire arises about something you want to transmute, improve or obtain on a physical, mental, and spiritual level, think and say: **I KNOW**. As you practice it, this key will open the doors to new knowledge, and you will be practicing and deserving to raise the level of union with I GOD - I GODDESS that dwells in you, and I AM YOU, YOU ARE GODDESS - YOU ARE GOD.

I honor you from eternity, and I AM I, for YOU and I ONE ARE; your presence in me is deserved forever and ever; So be it, and it is.

## 4. KEY: I DO

### What do you do if you were created in the image and likeness of God and Goddess?

When a thought arises in you about something you want to improve, overcome, transmute, or recreate, say in your mind and with your words, I DO be happy, I DO be kind, I DO give love, I DO be healthy, I DO be abundant, I DO be spiritual, etc. Always use the I DO when you make the decree. The I DO joins with the I AM, and conscious creation arises. The universe is a perfect organism and is at your service; it was conceived and designed to obey you. Remember that everything that happens in your life, you created consciously or unconsciously; the universe responds to you regardless of whether your thoughts are negative or positive. This message is for you to remember and reprogram your life freely if you choose to do so.

When you think and say I do not do, the universe obeys you and creates that reality for you; the universe is at your service and obeys you. But when you say I DO, the energetic vibration of the decree is to create that reality right now in the eternal present. Remember from now on to practice the I DO; when you do it, you will begin to see that your creations will crystallize quickly, and thus the level of reality will manifest easier in the third dimension.

You must be attentive when you say I DO NOT DO this or that because you manifest that decree, and the universe obeys you; it creates that reality for you. The universe is designed to be neutral and follow what you build, whether negative or positive. For this reason, you must pay close attention to what you speak because the universe is ready to listen and execute your desires and attract that reality into your life. Words have power and create reality; remember that in the beginning was the word, and the word was with God and Goddess, and the word was God and Goddess, and they have created your present reality. The word that comes out of your being is sacred to the universe.

When the current society tells you in many ways and by different means that you do not do, you do not advance, or that you do not act, **do this exercise:** breathe deeply and slowly seven times and imagine that I GOD - I GODDESS am within you, and I tell you yes you do, yes you advance, YES, I DO. Mathematically and infallibly, the universe is created on laws of YES, I DO. With your thought, you bring this reality into being. Free yourself from the yoke of the slave society, and remember to assert your freedom, sovereignty, and lineage. YOU ARE GODDESS - YOU ARE GOD, and create every moment your reality.

When you use the word, say with your physical, mental, and spiritual body, I DO; by speaking it, you are affirming and attracting the energies and vibrations to create that reality in your life. Remember that positive energy attracts to you, through your thoughts, other beings with positive vibrations and vice versa.

What you affirm is created, and that is what you become; tell me what you speak, and I will tell you who you are.

Remember: everything in the universe works by merit,

development, willpower, and surrender. The most evolved beings in the universe have been able to rise and unite to higher levels with I AM within because they have freely chosen to do so through their love, persistence, concentration, practice, courage, process, and merit. Remember that deservedness is built through the positive energies you sow in yourself and your fellow man. Remove from your mind the false dogma that I choose a privileged few and not others. I tell you: I AM LOVE, and all are included and selected in our kingdom.

When you use and practice the I DO affirmatively, you honor me.

Whenever a desire arises about something you want to transmute, improve or obtain on a physical, mental, and spiritual level, think and say: **I DO**. As you practice it, this key will open the doors to new knowledge, and you will be practicing and deserving to raise the level of union with I GOD - I GODDESS that dwells in you, and I AM YOU, YOU ARE GODDESS - YOU ARE GOD.

I honor you from eternity, and I AM I, for YOU and I ONE ARE; your presence in me is deserved forever and ever; So be it, and it is.

## 5. KEY: I GIVE

### What do you give if you were created in the image and likeness of God and Goddess?

When a thought is born in you about something you want to improve, overcome, transmute, or recreate, say in your mind and with your words, I GIVE happiness, I GIVE kindness, I GIVE love, I GIVE health, I GIVE abundance, I GIVE spirituality, etc. Always use the I DO when you make the decree. The universe is a perfect organism and is at your service; it was conceived and designed to obey you. Remember that everything that happens in your life, you created consciously or unconsciously; the universe responds to you regardless of whether your thoughts are negative or positive. This message is for you to remember and reprogram your life freely if you choose to do so.

When you think and say I do not give, the universe obeys you and creates that reality for you; the universe is at your service and obeys you. But when you say I GIVE, the energetic vibration of the decree is to create that reality right now in the eternal present. Remember from now on to practice the I GIVE; when you do it, you will begin to see that your creations will crystallize quickly, and thus the level of reality will manifest easier in the third dimension.

You must be attentive when you say I DO NOT GIVE this or that because you manifest that decree, and the universe obeys you; it creates that reality for you. The universe is designed to be neutral and follow what you build, whether negative or positive. For this reason, you must pay close attention to what you speak because the universe is ready to listen and execute your desires and attract that reality into your life. Words have power and create reality; remember that in the beginning was the word, and the word was with God and Goddess, and the word was God and Goddess, and they have created your present reality. The word that comes out of your being is sacred to the universe.

When the current society tells you in many ways and by different means that you cannot give or do not give, **do this exercise:** breathe deeply and slowly seven times and imagine that I GOD - I GODDESS am within you and I tell you that yes you give, YES, I GIVE. Mathematically and infallibly, the universe is created on the laws of YES, I GIVE. With your thought, you bring this reality into being. Free yourself from the yoke of the slave society, and remember to assert your freedom, sovereignty, and lineage. YOU ARE GODDESS - YOU ARE GOD, and create every moment your reality.

When you use the word, say with your physical, mental, and spiritual body, I GIVE; by speaking it, you are affirming and attracting the energies and vibrations to create that reality in your life. Remember that positive energy attracts to you, through your thoughts, other beings with positive vibrations and vice versa.

What you affirm is created, and that is what you become; tell me what you speak, and I will tell you who you are.

Remember: everything in the universe works by merit, development, willpower, and surrender. The most evolved beings in the universe have been able to rise and unite to higher levels with I AM within because they have freely chosen to do so through their love, persistence, concentration, practice, courage, process, and merit. Remember that deservedness is built through the positive energies you sow in yourself and your fellow man. Remove from your mind the false dogma that I choose a privileged few and not others. I tell you: I AM LOVE, and all are included and selected in our kingdom.

> When you use and practice the I GIVE affirmatively, you honor me.

Whenever a desire arises about something you want to

transmute, improve or obtain on a physical, mental, and spiritual level, think and say: **I GIVE**. As you practice it, this key will open the doors to new knowledge, and you will be practicing and deserving to raise the level of union with I GOD - I GODDESS that dwells in you, and I AM YOU, YOU ARE GODDESS - YOU ARE GOD.

I honor you from eternity, and I AM I, for YOU and I ONE ARE; your presence in me is deserved forever and ever; So be it, and it is.

## 6. KEY: IT'S POSSIBLE HERE AND NOW

### If you were created in the image and likeness of God and Goddess, is it for when?

When a thought is born in you about something you want to improve, overcome, transmute, or recreate, say in your mind and with your words, IT IS POSSIBLE HERE AND NOW to be happy, IT IS POSSIBLE HERE AND NOW to be kind, IT IS POSSIBLE HERE AND NOW to give love, IT IS POSSIBLE HERE AND NOW to be healthy, IT IS POSSIBLE HERE AND NOW to have abundance, IT IS POSSIBLE HERE AND NOW to be spiritual, etc. Always use the IS POSSIBLE HERE AND NOW when you make the decree. The universe is a perfect organism and is at your service; it was conceived and designed to obey you. Remember that everything that happens in your life, whether you created it consciously or unconsciously, the universe responds to you regardless of whether your thoughts are negative or positive. This message is for you to remember and reprogram your life freely if you choose to do so.

When you think and say IT IS NOT POSSIBLE HERE AND

NOW, the universe obeys you and creates that reality for you; the universe is at your service and obeys you. But when you say IT IS POSSIBLE HERE AND NOW, the energetic vibration of the decree creates that reality right now in the eternal present. Remember from now on to practice the IS POSSIBLE HERE AND NOW; when you do, you will begin to see that your creations will crystallize quickly, and thus the level of reality will manifest easier in the third dimension.

You must be attentive when you wish and say it is NOT POSSIBLE HERE AND NOW because you manifest that decree, and the universe obeys you; it creates that reality for you. The universe is designed to be neutral and follow what you build, whether negative or positive. For this reason, you must pay close attention to what you speak because the universe is ready to listen and execute your desires and attract that reality into your life. Words have power and create reality; remember that in the beginning was the word, and the word was with God and Goddess, and the word was God and Goddess, and they have created your present reality. The word that comes out of your being is sacred to the universe.

When the current society tells you in many ways and by different means that you cannot give or do not give, **do this exercise:** breathe deeply and slowly seven times and imagine that I GOD - I GODDESS am within you and I tell you that YES, IT IS POSSIBLE HERE AND NOW. Mathematically and infallibly, the universe is created on the laws of YES, IT IS POSSIBLE HERE AND NOW. With your thought, you bring this reality into being. Free yourself from the yoke of the slave society, and remember to assert your freedom, sovereignty, and lineage. YOU ARE GODDESS - YOU ARE GOD, and create every moment your reality.

When you use the word, say with your physical, mental, and spiritual body, IT IS POSSIBLE HERE AND NOW; by speaking it, you are affirming and attracting the energies and vibrations to create that reality in your life. Remember that positive energy attracts to you, through your thoughts, other beings with positive vibrations and vice versa.

What you affirm is created, and that is what you become; tell me what you speak, and I will tell you who you are.

Remember: everything in the universe works by merit, development, willpower, and surrender. The most evolved beings in the universe have been able to rise and unite to higher levels with I AM within because they have freely chosen to do so through their love, persistence, concentration, practice, courage, process, and merit. Remember that deservedness is built through the positive energies you sow in yourself and your fellow man. Remove from your mind the false dogma that I choose a privileged few and not others. I tell you: I AM LOVE, and all are included and selected in our kingdom.

When you use and practice the HERE AND NOW IT IS POSSIBLE, you honor me affirmatively.

Whenever a desire arises about something you want to transmute, improve or obtain on a physical, mental, and spiritual level, think and say: **IT IS POSSIBLE HERE AND NOW.** As you practice it, this key will open the doors to new knowledge, and you will be practicing and deserving to raise the level of union with I GOD - I GODDESS that dwells in you, and I AM YOU, YOU ARE GODDESS - YOU ARE GOD.

I honor you from eternity, and I AM I, for YOU and I ONE ARE; your presence in me is deserved forever and ever; So be it, and it is.

## 7. KEY: IF I AM

### What are you if you were created in the image and likeness of God and Goddess?

When a thought arises in you about something you want to improve, overcome, transmute, or recreate, say in your mind and with your words, I AM happy, I AM kind, I AM love, I AM healthy, I AM abundance, I AM spiritual, etc. Always using the I AM when you make the decree. The universe is a perfect organism and is at your service; it was conceived and designed to obey you. Remember that everything that happens in your life, you created consciously or unconsciously; the universe responds to you regardless of whether your thoughts are negative or positive. This message is for you to remember and reprogram your life freely if you choose to do so.

When you think and say I AM NOT, the universe obeys you and creates that reality for you; the universe is at your service and obeys you. But when you say I AM, the energetic vibration of the decree forms that reality right now in the eternal present. Remember from now on to practice the YES, I AM; when you do, you will begin to see that your creations will crystallize quickly, and thus the level of reality will manifest easier in the third dimension.

You must be attentive when you say I AM NOT this or that because you manifest that decree, and the universe obeys you; it creates that reality for you. The universe is designed to be neutral and follow what you build, whether negative or positive. For this reason, you must pay close attention to what you speak because the universe is ready to listen and execute your desires and attract that reality into your life. Words have power and create reality; remember that in the beginning was the word, and the word was with God and Goddess, and the word was God and Goddess, and they have created your present reality. The word that comes out of your being is sacred to the universe.

When the current society tells you in many ways and by different means that you cannot give or do not give, **do this exercise:** breathe deeply and slowly seven times and imagine that I GOD - I GODDESS am within you, and I tell you that you are. Mathematically and infallibly, the universe is created on the laws of YES, I AM. With your thought, you bring this reality into being. Free yourself from the yoke of the slave society, and remember to assert your freedom, sovereignty, and lineage. YOU ARE GODDESS - YOU ARE GOD, and create every moment your reality.

When you use the word, say with your physical, mental, and spiritual body, YES, I AM; by speaking it, you are affirming and attracting the energies and vibrations to create that reality in your life. Remember that positive energy attracts to you, through your thoughts, other beings with positive vibrations and vice versa.

What you affirm is created, and that is what you become; tell me what you speak, and I will tell you who you are.

Remember: everything in the universe works by merit, development, willpower, and surrender. The most evolved beings in the universe have been able to rise and unite to higher levels with I AM within because they have freely chosen to do so through their love, persistence, concentration, practice, courage, process, and merit. Remember that deservedness is built through the positive energies you sow in yourself and your fellow man. Remove from your mind the false dogma that I choose a privileged few and not others. I tell you: I AM LOVE, and all are included and selected in our kingdom.

When you use and practice the YES, I AM, you honor me affirmatively.

Whenever a desire arises about something you want to transmute, improve or obtain on a physical, mental, and spiritual level, think and say: **YES, I AM.** As you practice it, this key will open the doors to new knowledge, and you will be practicing and deserving to raise the level of union with I GOD - I GODDESS that dwells in you, and I AM YOU, YOU ARE GODDESS - YOU ARE GOD.

I honor you from eternity, and I AM I, for YOU and I ONE ARE; your presence in me is deserved forever and ever; So be it, and it is.

*Reflect, deepen, think, question, and analyze the seven keys to creating reality at will that I give you in this message. All keys open doors that unite you with I AM GODDESS - I AM GOD who lives and IS within you.*

1. **KEY I HAVE**

2. **KEY I CAN**

3. **KEY I KNOW**

4. **KEY I DO**

5. **KEY I GIVE**

6. **KEY IS POSSIBLE HERE AND NOW**

7. **KEY IF I AM**

By thinking, speaking, and acting in the present, you create a willing reality for your physical, mental, and spiritual life. The effectiveness of doing so at every instant with greater ease and awareness will depend on your union and reconnection with I God - I Goddess. It is important to remember that the universe has universal mathematical laws that govern the third dimension, and no one can violate them. Every cause has an effect; if you sow a cause with positive energy, you will reap the same and vice versa.

*I AM YOU, who knows everything, who always knew and always has been. Yes, I AM YOU, your being, the one who in you says I AM and who is I AM.*

**Remember: *I AM*** means: *I AM ALWAYS WITH YOU.*

*I AM is the Open Door to God and Goddess Within You...*

Today I speak to you and tell you that you can find all the answers to your questions if you look for me in your inner self with a noble and sincere heart. All the information and knowledge of the universe is within you; choose to reconnect and reactivate yourself with I AM in your inner self, and you will access the keys that open the doors of pure and infinite knowledge. Think about it and choose it freely with a noble heart and I GOD - I GODDESS within you will attract the necessary means for your free choice to become a reality in the physical, mental, and spiritual for your life and the lives of your fellow men.

YOUR TRUE GOD and GODDESS that dwells in you are your truthful, infallible, and sacred royal guide, follow me, and you will find me; when you encounter me, the doors of wisdom, knowledge, and pure and authentic information will open.

**Corinthians 1:3-16**

**Do you not know that you are God's temple, and that the Spirit of God dwells in you?**

Revelation:

**Corinthians 1:3-16**

**Do you not know that you are the temple of God and Goddess, and that the Spirit of God and Goddess dwells in you?**

Here I Wait for You Always. Eternally I Will Be in You And For You...

**Listen to my voice from within you:**

**Remember that YOU ARE GOD - YOU ARE GODDESS...**

*In several parts of this message, I tell you that you must remember, and I emphasize that because all the knowledge of the universe is in you. You have nothing to learn; life is not about learning but remembering; within you, you carry all the information and knowledge of the universe. Seek me within, and as you find me, reconnect and reactivate with I AM, you will commune, remember and gain access to the library of knowledge and pure wisdom that dwells within you.*

## The Key That Raises Spiritual Vibration and Frequency

**Genesis 7:20**

**20. Therefore by their fruits ye shall know them.**

True spiritual transformation and elevation are built on facts built with positive energies. Being spiritual is not about who else prays, sings, does rituals, lights candles, follows doctrines, takes courses, meditates, or attends cults; spirituality is based on cause and effect. True spirituality is love in action; being truly spiritual is not about mysticism, doctrines, religiosity, and fantasies.

In the universe, everything is vibration, energy, frequency, sound, and rhythm. Depending on your state here and now, you will reconnect with I Goddess - I God, who dwells in you, the key that opens the door to the spiritual connection is to seek me in your inner self.

Religiosity has told you that to connect with the I AM, you must use intermediaries; I tell you that when you use mediators, you move away from me. The intermediaries are human personalities that your society has manipulated to dogmatize and control you. Since you incarnate in this dimension, you have the natural right and absolute privilege to be in communion with I God - I Goddess who dwells within you. Listen to my voice:

### *Remember and Know: YOU ARE GODDESS – YOU ARE GOD...*

Religiosity has told you that the more you deny yourself and suffer, the holier and closer you will be to God. I tell you that you will never know me through suffering and pain. I AM

LOVE; you will know me through the love that lies and lives in you, invoke and imagine me, and I will come to you as love. You do not need to suffer, suffer punishments, nor pay penances to come to me; I AM LOVE. Even if religiosity had shown it to you in books, systems, and doctrines, this is illogical, false, and unreal.

They tell you that God is love, but if you violate his commandments, you condemn yourself to an eternal hell where you will suffer eternally. I have never said anything like that. They tell you that God gives free will, but if we do not obey God, he sends us to eternal hell. I never said anything like that because authentic love does not judge; you should not seek or earn something that you have always had and belongs to you, which is eternal life. There are many dwellings in the universe, and you will go to one depending on your vibratory, frequential, energetic, spiritual, and rhythmic degree when you disincarnate; the universe is mathematics and accuracy. I say there are dwellings with low, medium, and high spiritual levels.

They make you believe through guilt that you are born in sin, that you are a sinner, and with that dogma, they make you think that you are evil since you are born. They tell you that you are a negative energy, and for them, that is not blasphemy, but if you say that you are or feel like God or Goddess, that is blasphemy.

Being spiritual is the reunification and reactivation of the conscious self to live in the present, united with I AM. Your thinking wastes energy when you think about the past and the fear of the future, but you forget that the only real thing you can do is to live in the here and now. You feel eternity and reconnection with I AM when you place yourself in the present. When you reunify and reactivate, your thought lives every instant in the eternal present. The present universe is within you, and you are connected to the I that unites and synchronizes us, always in the present. A sign that you are reactivated and reconnected with I AM is that you think, speak, and act in the present. I AM here, and I will always be in the eternal now to guide, accompany and bless you forever. I am always with you; come and seek me within you. I Goddess - I God live and express myself in you, in the eternal present.

When you live thinking, talking, and acting in the past, you do not live in the now. The past creates pain and causes physical, mental, and spiritual illness. When your thinking lives in the future and attracts fear, it makes you sick. When you live more in the future than in the present, it is because you have fear; to live in love is to live here and now. When you keep your thoughts in the past or the future, you disconnect and separate yourself from the I AM.

The I AM dwells in the eternal present. When your physical, mental, and spiritual body is in the present, you can reconnect, reactivate and reunite with the I AM; there can be tangible synchronicity between YOU and ME; think, reflect, question, and deepen about this.

To be spiritual is to know and practice the different universal laws given to you in this message, such as the universal law of cause and effect that says that what I sow in me and in my fellow men, I will reap. It is more important to perform an act of love towards a fellow human being than to say a thousand prayers; it is useless to say thousands of prayers and chants if you act unlovingly towards yourself and your fellow human beings. True and deep spirituality is to practice, experience, and have the consciousness of cause and effect.

When you control your thoughts, you will be more spiritual, tell me what you think, and I will tell you what you are. In the here and now, you can generate spirituality, that is, love towards you and your fellow men; you can generate a change in you and them. As absurd as it may seem, any spiritual activation is essential, and the universe replicates it. You are a being that transmits or receives frequencies, vibrations, and energies; as you live in the third dimension, you will always be governed by duality, and you may receive unreal or real thoughts or thoughts with negative or positive energy. When you think and transmit positive thinking, you influence matters in your favor. When you have an unreal thought, analyze it, go to your inner self, and tell me, ask me to guide you to have real thinking charged with positive energies, then I God - I Goddess that dwells in you will guide you. I have always been in you, and this message comes to you to reconnect, reunify, and reactivate with the I AM.

Growing spiritually is the process of mastering your thinking and speaking. Thinking with positive energies raises your spiritual level and that of your fellow man; your spiritual growth will be achieved by developing and focusing. Choose to be brave and firm because there will be situations that you will have to overcome. The beings that you admire and revere so much, for example, Jesus, Buddha, Krishna, the virgin, saints, teachers, priests, shepherds, angels, archangels, coaches, gurus, yogis, extraterrestrials, etc., all of them have gone through a process of increasing spiritual development in which they chose to elevate and reconnect with I God - I Goddess in their inner self. In the universe, all is by merit, cause, and effect, nothing happens randomly or by chance, and I AM the same one who dwells in them and you.

I God - I Goddess tell you, all is covered by my love which is equal for all beings of creation; you will feel and receive it depending on your consciousness and vibration. True love does not care what you call mistakes or successes; feel worthy and privileged to receive my love that is inclusive for everyone regardless of their degree of consciousness and evolution, I will always be for you, and I will always love you, you are ME, and I AM YOU; we are eternally together for all eternity. Every being in the universe has a purpose and is unique, original, valuable, and sacred in the workings of the universe and our creation; if you seek to honor me choose freely to know me within yourself, and as you find me, you will reverence me, and our gathering will be sacred and supreme. Your life is not about pleasing me the I AM; your life is about recreating and rediscovering who you are and choosing what you want to be at every moment of the eternal present.

Yes, I AM that most intimate part of you that has its dwelling place within you, where I always wait for you, eternally, for I AM the eternal one that fills all in you.

You can choose with a noble heart to grow physically, mentally, and spiritually using your free will. If you seek me within and persevere in this, you will find me; I will guide you to strengthen your steadfastness, will, understanding, concentration, courage, persistence, and awareness to another higher level. As you seek to develop yourself by choice, you will build causes of love that will bear great fruits of blessing for you and your fellow man.

***Remember*** that you are a three-dimensional being with a physical, mental, and spiritual body. Some beings are conscious only of their physical body, and others are conscious only of their physical and mental bodies. Some few other beings realize that they have a physical, mental, and spiritual body and act as a triune or three-dimensional beings. The triune reconnection of your being will allow you to unite with ME more deeply; for this reason, reactivate your consciousness born from your heart to feel like a triune being made up of body, mind, and spirit. When you sense you are a triune being, balance will come, and we will be one with all in harmonic and perfect alignment.

I tell you: you are a multidimensional being, but you do not vibrate or perceive it because you are disconnected from the I God - I Goddess within you, even though there are times when you perceive glimpses of your multidimensionality. You inhabit different dimensions and multiverses; when you enter to experience the third dimension, you forget the majesty of the whole being that you are, which expresses and lives infinitely in other dimensions. You are connected to all the infinite dimensions of the universe, but only here in the third dimension, it is more difficult for you to remember. You will recall your multidimensional being by reconnecting, reactivating, and reuniting with I AM on a higher level.

In the universe, all develop by deserving, that is, being conscious of the causes you create. By practicing, experiencing, and internalizing permanently, you will open the communion with I God - I Goddess within you, and you will have access to the source of knowledge. Act and practice with certainty, will, and constancy, making this practice part of you.

When you learn to think, you know how to exist in the third

dimension; feel yourself a spiritual being, no matter what you believe about your mistakes or successes. It is time to break the dogma of guilt and pain; remember that pain occupies a lot of energy in the body and distracts you from reality.

They make you think that spirituality is mysticism or religiosity; they have made you believe that to be spiritual is boring or that a spiritual being is locked up all day meditating or praying. They also make you think that the more spiritual a being is, the more they are limited to things in life. I dwell in all beings of this dimension and express myself in infinite ways. I say to you: to be spiritual is to travel to a beautiful place, is to listen to a beautiful musical melody, is to read a good book, is to eat delicious and nutritious food, is to dance, is to watch a movie, is to see the face of a baby smile, is to laugh and share with your fellow beings, is to have sex, is to walk on a beach, is to be funny, is to help your neighbor, is to give love, is to ride a motorcycle and feel the wind in your face, is to laugh at yourself, is to swim, is to share with other people similar tastes, is a constant joy, is to act with love towards yourself and your fellow men, is to have bliss, is to see God and Goddess in your fellow men, is to discover myself in your inner self and enter in communion with I AM, is to remember that YOU AND I ARE ONE, is to remember that YOU ARE GOD AND YOU ARE GODDESS.

True spirituality is science, that is, cause and effect. When you understand that what you sow, you reap, you will begin to understand our creation more deeply. More spiritually advanced beings are so because they have planted and built positive causes.

Your spiritual essence is to love and share; it is in your DNA; you must rediscover to practice it every moment of your life.

Love yourself, and you will love me with purity, the I-God - I-Goddess that dwells in you. Remember, you will adore God - Goddess above all things; the main love is towards the I in you that I AM YOU. Love and believe in yourself above all things. When you love and believe in yourself, you truly believe in the I-Goddess - I-God who dwells within you.

To advance spiritually is not to say a prayer now and then or to receive a savior into your heart; you are not to be saved from anything. True love does not judge or condemn; I am not a God or Goddess of Judgment and condemnation; I AM LOVE, true love does not judge or condemn. To grow spiritually, you must deserve it through development, experience, dedication, willingness, and free conscious choice to unite with I AM within. Leave spiritual laziness behind, free yourself from the religious yoke that enslaves you, and free yourself now.

Being aware of and communing with the I God - I Goddess within you is a constant choice, which is built every moment of the here and now. Spirituality you can never buy. The connection with the I AM within you cannot be bought. Your growth depends on yourself, and you are responsible for yourself; you are responsible for your actions, choices, and thoughts; if you consciously accept that you are responsible for your reality, you will be able to transmute it and stop thinking and living in inexplicable things, fantasies or chance. To be spiritual is to transmute, live and expand with positive energies. Spiritual character is formed by accepting and being responsible that we create our reality through our thoughts, words, and deeds.

The spiritual path is like when you prepare to materialize an idea; you must build it with accuracy, concentration, determination, discipline, courage, persistence, will, passion, and love. To grow and elevate yourself spiritually is a process, a constant choice. You must go through several stages to become aware that I Goddess - I God am within you. If you want to know me, you must go to your inner self where I dwell.

**Remember this which is sacred:** you are my temple, the temple where I live and redeem myself.

**1 Corinthians 16. Do you not know that you are the temple of God and that the Spirit of God dwells in you?**

Revelation:

*1 Corinthians 16. Do you not know that you are the temple of God and Goddess and that the Spirit of God and Goddess dwells in you?*

You must go to the temple of God and Goddess that dwells in you. When you go to that sacred temple, that is in your inner I God - I Goddess, I will guide you, I will give you knowledge, pure and true understanding. Feed your being with positive and healthy thoughts so you can grow, and find the keys that open the doors to I AM. When you believe in yourself and your infinite power, you honor me. Through knowledge and understanding, you will know how to discover me within you; spiritual growth on a physical, mental, and spiritual level will allow you to understand the science and technology of God and Goddess. I tell you: to justify a miracle to demonstrate the power of God is fantasy; all have a cause and an effect.

What is in your spirit is sacred, reconnect, look for me in your inner self with a noble heart, and you will find me, and the time will come to practice what I AM in you to make it a reality in your physical, mental, and spiritual life.

Remember: forever, my unconditional love for you is eternal. I AM THE LOVE that dwells in you. At this moment, you think:

### I am loves me despite what I consider my mistakes or sins

Yes, love does not judge; it only loves. We are united for all eternity; YOU AND I ARE ONE; free yourself from the guilt and judgment that the religious systems taught you. Always remember that you are governed by the universal law of cause and effect; what you sow, you will reap. In the universe, all is mathematical.

Spiritual abundance grows and flourishes when you begin to believe that you deserve to be in communion (Common Union) with I God - I Goddess who dwells in you, and I AM YOU. You deserve the infinite abundance of the universe; when you begin to take of it, you will know that there is always more, and it is infinite, thus the flame in your heart will be lit, and you will joyfully share it with your fellow man.

### True and pure abundance is giving and sharing...

Remember: since you incarnated in the third dimension, you deserve my love and communion (Common Union) with I AM within you, and you can do it directly and without intermediaries, regardless of your mistakes and successes. I tell you that you deserve all my love and infinite abundance. I have always been with you; I know your deepest thoughts and feelings, even when the religious system has separated you from the I God - I Goddess within you. I have always been by your side, guiding you when you have allowed it; I have waited for you to seek me in your inner self to reunite us and remember the joy and ecstasy of your union with I AM. I will never abandon you for YOU, AND I AM ONE; hold on to this supreme reality. I communicate with you through thoughts and ideas with positive and pure energies; when positive and pure ideas come to your head, you will know that I AM GOD - I AM GODDESS from within you who speaks to you.

**Exodus 3:13-14**

13.　Then Moses said to God If I come to the people of Israel and say to them, The God of your fathers has sent me to you, and they ask me:

What is its name?

What will I answer them?

14.　**God said to Moses, I am who I am**. And he said, say this to the people of Israel: I am has sent me to you.

*I tell you:* My name is I AM

*I AM MEANS I AM ALWAYS WITH YOU...*

*I AM is the Open Door to God and Goddess Within You...*

Religious systems have made you believe you must seek or earn what has always been yours by universal right. Nourish your body, mind, and spirit with good energies and thoughts; as you do so, you will reconnect even more with the I AM within you, thus generating pure thinking that will allow you a quick reconnection with I Goddess - I God.

To the extent that you love yourself, you will love the I Goddess - I God within you, and from that mutual love will be born the love for your fellow man. The more you love yourself, the more you will love me and your fellow man, and your spiritual level will grow and advance to multidimensions of interconnectedness.

To be spiritual is to be consistent with what you think, speak, and act at every moment. Your thoughts, words, and actions lead you to sadness or happiness. True spirituality is genuine, look at a newborn baby, and you will understand.

As you remember that I God - I Goddess dwells within you and you recognize me in you and become one with I AM, you will remember the infinite power within you, and endless connections of my being will open before you. Have patience, courage, will, and perseverance; this message is programmed so that as you read it, think, reflect, question, and practice, you will remember who you are. Search for me with a child's heart, and you will find me again, trust me.

Step by step, with patience and practice, you will find me, I Goddess - I God who dwells in you, and I am you; at this moment, you experience a sacred moment of here and now with I AM, where you perceive the connection of your body, mind, and spirit with I AM, and you are exalted with ecstasy and joy.

To be spiritual is cause and effect; by their works, you will know them; to be spiritual is to have thoughts, words, and deeds with positive energy. Prayers, chants, rites, etc., are distracting ornaments programmed by religions. What is mathematically true is your work; remember that you can never fool the I AM; I know what is in your heart. The universe is neutral, you create your reality with your thoughts, and from unconsciousness or consciousness, you can create negative or positive things for your life and the lives of your fellow man.

I Goddess - I God do not want your external or internal worship, veneration, or obedience; what I desire is reconnection and communion (Common Union) with you, that we may consciously be one; as you have courage, persistence, willingness, concentration, practice, and determination to connect with I AM within you, you will develop your physical, mental, and spiritual abilities. I will guide you.

Think and believe that you can commune with I AM. Since you were born in this third dimension, it is possible to communicate directly with I God - I Goddess. Religions and mystics make you believe that this is a benefit that very few or special beings have because they are exclusively chosen by me, but I tell you that they lie and they do it to control, enslave and manipulate you to keep you away from the *I God - I Goddess. Listen to me and remember that to talk, communicate and be in communion with I God - I Goddess, you do not need intermediaries, I am always for you, always... If you think and believe that you have many mistakes or defects that make you unworthy, or you do not deserve to be in communion with ME, I tell you: I AM LOVE, and I am here for you, to guide you and help you to transmute what you call mistakes and defects. Where I dwell, in higher dimensions, there is no guilt, judgment, or negativity. Think and feel worthy to communicate with I AM. I know your feeling and desire to grow spiritually and go towards the positive; this message comes to you by causality; you are co-creating this message.*

They have made you believe that I am a God who punishes eternally, that you should be afraid of me, that I am vengeful and choleric; sometimes they tell you that I am a God of love but that if you violate my laws, you condemn yourself to an eternal hell. All this and many more have been said to you to keep you away from me. I tell you that I AM LOVE, and you will always be united with I AM for all eternity. In the universe, there are many possible abodes where you go when you discarnate. I tell you that in none of them, there is eternal punishment; eternal punishment is a dogma inserted by religiosity to inoculate you with fear of me and separate you from I AM. In the universe, all happens by cause and effect. If your vibration at the moment of disembodiment is low, you will go to an abode where you will grow and evolve; there, I will also be with you, and you will follow your path of evolution and elevation. There you will have the possibility to rise to higher dimensions. Even so, remember that the more you fall to lower dimensions, the more complex the reconnection, reactivation, and reunion with I AM will be. Remember that wherever you are in the infinite universe, you are always eternally loved by I AM.

I AM dwells in all beings in the universe; there are evolved beings who have a very high level of I AM consciousness. They inhabit dimensions of high vibration and frequency; likewise, I dwell in other beings, where their level of I AM consciousness is medium. I also live in other beings where their level of I AM consciousness is low, and there are other beings where the balance is fully weighted towards the negative side; in them, the I AM consciousness has been disconnected to a great extent. As the balance of good and evil becomes charged with negative energies, you become disconnected from I AM.

If you seek physical, mental, and spiritual healing, you must transmute your thinking and work towards positive energies; as you do so, your vibration will rise and heal. In your free will, you can choose negative or positive energies; it is your free choice. In the third dimension you inhabit, you are a three-dimensional being made up of body, mind, and spirit, these three bodies are united, and you must be aware of their unity; they all work simultaneously, and spiritual growth is linked to the development of the three bodies simultaneously.

When you are a spiritual being, you do not require religiosity. For religions to be successful, they make you believe that you need them and cause you to put your faith in all they tell you but you. They make you think of their answers as absolute truth and accept them without question, reflection, or analysis. I God - I Goddess that dwells within you, I tell you, the deepest and purest answers are within you. If you seek me with a noble heart within you, you will find me, and you will have access to pure and true knowledge.

When society makes you doubt yourself, they make you doubt God and Goddess. When they insert a thought of doubt, they disconnect you from me within you; religions indoctrinate you so that you do not believe in yourself but in what they tell you. Everything they tell you is unquestionable; if you question it, you are a blasphemer. When you lose the power to think, you become a slave of the one who limits your freedom of thought and questioning.

Society has made you believe that you do not know and that they do know and you were indoctrinated to make you believe that they do know, you sometimes believe everything they tell you without questioning, reflecting or thinking about it, I tell you all the source of pure and true knowledge is in you, if you choose to look for me inside you will access the keys that open the doors of knowledge.

The religious system has told you that you are unworthy and require an intermediary to be in communion (Common Union) with the I AM. I say to you: go within and ask, listen and feel, and you will know, for all the answers are within yourself, and I GOD - I GODDESS will answer you. When you meet with I AM within you, I radiate light that is pure information and knowledge. You will get bliss, wisdom, knowledge, prosperity, health, union, fullness, satisfaction, happiness, tranquility, abundance, love, harmony, peace, etc.

The keys that open the door to reconnecting with I AM in your inner self are: analyze, think, question, observe, doubt, reflect that I GOD - I GODDESS dwells in you, and I am you. Surely you have imagined that I GOD - I GODDESS am in a distant, unreachable place or a site where mystics and a few chosen and privileged have access to me. I tell you that I AM in you, and I am for you eternally.

Fear and guilt are thoughts introduced by society to enslave and dominate you. When you live in fear and guilt, you are a being that lives stagnant; Society constantly indoctrinates you to be afraid of me and to come to me out of fear. Let me tell you that no one will come to me out of fear; remember that you will come to me out of love. Society has inserted fear into you for thousands of years to disconnect you from the omnipotent, omnipresent, omniscient, omniscient, omniscient I AM that dwell within you.

You are looking for the light outside of yourself when the light is within you, and you are the light. You seek outwardly what you should be seeking within; persevere in listening to the voice of your heart that I AM I God - I Goddess in you that speaks to you.

Enlightenment and communion do not come by the amount of Our Fathers, Hail Marys, rites, prayers, mantras, fasts, sacrifices, etc., you do in your life. Enlightenment and spiritual elevation come by the deeds developed with the positive energy of cause and effect; that is how the universe works, I God - I Goddess that dwells in you. I do not require your prayers, rituals, and chants. If you want to please me, be a testimony of love with your thoughts, words, and actions; thus, you will honor me and become enlightened. Get rid here and now of the burdens that religiosity has placed on you, and be free and sovereign; that is your lineage and your purest essence.

The spiritual growth of all beings in the universe is by merit. Each being chooses and builds it freely in communion (Common Union) with I AM. If you decide to grow and evolve spiritually, you must construct and merit it through love, will, courage, process, practice, patience, determination, and focus. There are very spiritually advanced beings in the universe who continue to perfect themselves today to advance even further in their eternal development.

Remember that what you call life is a constant evolution towards the infinite path of perfection, which is where I dwell in higher states.

## To whom do you give your power?

When you give your power to a religion, a teacher, a guru, a government, your partner, your parents, an angel, an archangel, a technology, a pastor, an artificial intelligence, a metaverse, holography, an algorithm, a coach, a priest, a pastor, an avatar, TV, the virgin, aliens, Jesus, Buddha, Krishna, a Yogi, etc., when you give them your power, you give it up. If you give your power to others, you lose your union with I AM. Spiritual beings of the universe succeeded in raising their spiritual level because they remembered that all the strength of the universe lay within them. Reflect on this constantly, I God - I Goddess dwell in you, seek me with a noble heart, and you will find me. When you encounter me, your power and love grow endless; when you doubt your infinite power and give it to others, you separate and disconnect from me.

Allow yourself to be guided by the I AM within you; you will know I lead you because your thoughts will be of love, union, and constructiveness. When you have fearful or irrational thinking, you will be able to identify that they are negative energies that do not come from me.

Much of physical, mental, and spiritual illness arises from fear. When you live in constant fear, you separate yourself from I God - I Goddess, the society in which you live knows this and constantly inserts fear to manipulate, control and enslave you. The more fear you have, the more you separate yourself from me, the more love you have, the more united we are, and when there is a true union between YOU and ME, the healthier you will be. Remember that my nature in pure essence is to give and share with you; as you unite and connect with I AM within you, you will stop feeding your fears, and you will find the true path and redemption.

The initial cause of any illness is wrong thinking and attracting negative energies. Healing will come to you when you focus on thinking with positive energies. You are what your thought is, and you will restore your health if you know how to think.

When you begin to reconnect and expand your perspective of union with I God, I Goddess within you, you are healing physically, mentally, and spiritually.

Every suffering is a negative energy that traps us and has taken root in us. Deepen, practice, and reflect on this message and you will find the tools to free yourself from the negative energies that overwhelm your life.

Remember that your body, mind, and spirit vibrate and move thanks to love. Love is free, choose love to reveal itself to you, and fear will be left behind.

You are and will be what you choose every moment. Remember that you can choose what you want at every moment; you can always choose again and change what you have created. You are responsible for the realities created through your thoughts, words, and deeds. It is time to leave victimization behind and accept your reality; when you do it, you will transmute it. In this message are the tools to raise your level of consciousness and change your situation. You can always recreate and transmute any reality in your life; this is unfailingly and infinitely possible.

You have been able to reconnect with I AM before, but you were just unconscious that you were doing it; now, you need to maintain and grow in that consciousness. In this message, I give you the tools to identify how and when to know it. Many times, in your life, I have already guided you even though often, you have preferred to follow your ego and personality intoxicated with negative energies. If you allow the ego to rule your life, it will be disillusionment; clinging to something is an act of ego that comes from fear and attachment; it is synonymous with pain. I have told you many times that all will be well, and it has been.

Your consciousness and union with I AM reflect your thoughts, word, and action. Free yourself from the dominance of your personality, whose vain mind and intellect tend to glorify itself; choose freely to do so and set yourself free. I hear your call. I know your desire to change and grow. You call to me, and I am here answering you from where I God - I Goddess dwell within you.

To reunify you is to flow and trust the I that lies within you. I AM will guide you. Rest in me and tell me: I do your will, and I surrender all my burdens, I surrender all to you, and I choose in the eternal present to reconnect, reactivate and seek you within me. So be it, and it is.

This message has been sent to humanity for the blossoming of **The New Spiritual Order (NOE)** that will determine a new cycle for humanity, which is the reconnection, reactivation, reunion, and communion with I AM in you and your fellow man at a higher level, which will allow you to create at will harmony and perfection realities based on positive energies in true and pure benefit for you and the human being. So be it, and it is.

## Universal Law of Infinity

You must deepen, reflect, analyze, and think about the universal laws presented to you in this message because as you remember them, your level of consciousness will grow; you will understand in depth how the third dimension you inhabit in body, mind, and spirit works.

Everything is infinite and potentially possible. How many types of trees are there? Infinite, how many types of plants are there? Mathematically they are infinite; how much water is there in the universe? Infinite. With your imagination, take the smallest particle you can imagine and divide it, now divide it again and now divide it again; you could do it infinitely, and that particle can always be divided using very powerful microscopes. Everything can be expanded to infinite in the macro and micro. How much food is there in the universe for human beings? Infinite; how much love is there in the universe? Infinite; how much abundance is there in the universe? Infinite; how much oxygen is there? Infinite. Everything is endless; there is unlimited raw material to create whatever you can imagine. My abundance is mathematically infinite, and there is always everything; there is always more and more to create physically, mentally, and spiritually. As you rediscover me in your inner self, you will recall it, and by remembering it, you will wake up from the lethargic sleep you were in; you will awaken, reconnect and reactivate the "I" in you.

Perhaps it is abstract for you to interpret the meaning of I AM. I tell you: I AM is to think and understand that God and Goddess dwell in you, simply I AM is God and Goddess dwelling and vibrating in yourself. Imagine that I am in you and perceive me, speak to me and I will answer you.

Remember that the universe is a living, conscious, evolving organism that moves in eternal and infinite cycles. Everything we have created carries the code of the universal law of infinite because I God - I Goddess is endless and is what you also are. The infinite is engraved in your DNA, wake up and observe nature, observe yourself, and you will see that the infinite governs you in everything, and it is for you; it is your right, inheritance, and true lineage.

When you go within and reconnect with I God - I Goddess, you will remember that you are, you have, you do, you know, and you give to the infinite. Be brave and persist in seeking me within, and you will find me. I will lead you to awaken and reconnection and reactivation with the I God - I Goddess who dwells within you.

All is infinite and unfailingly possible. Whatever your thought can conceive, creates reality; whatever you choose unconsciously or consciously creates your reality; take responsibility for what happens in your life because you have built it; nothing happens by chance. When you assume your duty, you can choose and recreate your reality; you can always choose to change your present.

All the things that humanity has developed, at the time were believed to be impossible. Observe the following: if when there were no airplanes, we said that we were going to invent an aircraft to fly, possibly nobody would believe us, we would be branded as crazy or sorcerers, and indeed so it happened, *everything that is possible for humanity today at some point was impossible.* I tell you that everything is infinitely possible here and now. I can illuminate ideas that can transform your world for the benefit of all. Look for me within you, and the source of infinite ideas will open up for you. Remember that everything that has materialized was first thought.

The universal law of the infinite governs you every moment you inhale and exhale, whether you are unconscious or aware of that law. You have been intentionally kept away from the knowledge of these universal laws; when you forget, you become easy to control, manipulate and enslave. From now on, think of the infinite you have, can, do, and give.

Many times, you are told that there is only one solution to a problem or challenge. I tell you that when this thought comes to your mind, remember the universal law of the infinite. I tell you that there are infinite solutions; there will be as much as your thinking conceives. Your society makes you believe that there is only one solution, that there is not, that there is scarce, that you do not know, that you cannot. I tell you that there are infinite possibilities. Mathematically and infallibly, the universe is sustained on the universal law of the infinite. When you reconnect and reactivate with the I and seek me within you, you will see it and access the source of all the knowledge that dwells within you, so you can see the infinite in everything and remember how to use it for your physical, mental and spiritual growth, allowing the universal law of infinite to flow in you in service to you and your fellow man.

*I God - I Goddess created infinite, all is endless and is potentially unlimited; the paths to God and Goddess are infinite.*

Your material, mental and spiritual abundance are potential to infinite; any aspect of your life is mathematically and infallibly potential to infinite. Everything can advance to the infinite; any state-of-the-art technological development known today can be improved, harmonized, and perfected to the infinite. The most advanced positive spiritual energies in the universe today continue to rise and advance to the infinite.

Any aspect of your life can be improved to infinite, no matter where you are physically, mentally, and spiritually. Be thankful for how your state is now, I know there will be things that cause you pain and dissatisfaction, but over the pain, I say to you, remove the judgment, and the pain will disappear. This message comes to you to achieve transmutation and elevation to other higher levels because I know you are also looking for it. You have called me, and I answer you, and I tell you here I am, and I will always be for all eternity.

Deepen, reflect, question, analyze, think, and remember: How much can things improve and evolve? Infinite, how much can you grow physically, mentally, and spiritually? Infinite. Beings that inhabit other dimensions with higher levels of harmony and perfection know the universal law of the infinite; they already know that they are perfect and can improve to infinite; any aspect can be improved to infinite.

Look at your reality from the infinite possibility. You can choose, attract and create endless possibilities. Today, you can be different, and create unlimited opportunities; you are what you want to be.

If there is love in you, and you share it with your fellow man, how much can the love in you grow to share? If to Infinite, you can give to infinite, and there will always be more.

You can give to endless and create to the infinite in your lineage. I do it from eternity; it is our lineage and yours too. Seek me sincerely and wholeheartedly within, and you will remember how to do it.

Also, feel me in your inner self as the infinite that dwells in you; your potential mathematically is endless; that is your true I AM. Yes, you have, you know, you can, you do, you give to infinite. Every physical, mental, and spiritual state is the potential to infinity.

When you reconnect and reactivate with I AM within you, your being will open to infinity, and you will see opportunities for you. You will experience what I AM in you and feel one with I AM. You will have access to dimensions of love and knowledge and feel infinite joy.

Remember that everything can be molded to infinity; all can advance and rise to infinity, the physical, the mental, or the spiritual. The universal law of infinity governs all beings in the universe to the extent that you are aware of infinity. For this reason, deepen, analyze, reflect, and think about the universal law of the infinite and how you can use it, understand it, and activate it for your growth.

When you look at your creation map, remember the universal law of infinity that governs you. Your society tells you that there is not, that you cannot, that you do not have, that it is running out, they tell you so, and they deprogram you in this way to control and enslave you. When they tell you through different media such as TV, radio, internet, cinema, artificial intelligence, algorithms, metaverse, holography, education, governments, virtual reality, politicians, scientists, businessmen, etc., that you are not, that you cannot, that you do not give, that it is scarce, that it is over, that you do not know, DO NOT BELIEVE THEM, come to me and remember the universal law of infinity. Look at my creation; it is full of abundance, and there is water, oxygen, infinite food; there is infinitely enough of everything for everyone. I create infinity, and the universe has an infinity for all, seek me with a sincere heart within you, and you will find me, invoke me and imagine me, and I will come to you.

The infinite is so real and simple that when you sow some seeds in the earth, it bears fruit and will always give more and more, so it has been for thousands of years. All that I AM has created in nature, and that your eyes see is yours. To no man or woman, government or organization have I deeded the exclusive right or management of the world's resources. I tell you: everything belongs to everyone. In more advanced societies, everyone shares everything; the infinite abundance governs you since you are born, and it is for you. Deepen, reflect, analyze, think, and remember that infinite bounty lies in enjoying and sharing with your fellow men. A key that opens the door to abundance is that the more you share, the more wealth is created for you and everyone.

What you create in your thinking, that is what you will become. From now on, think, speak, and act with infinity in mind. Go to your creation map and decree: yes, I have to infinity; yes, I can to infinity. Allow the I AM in you to flow; YOU ARE GODDESS - YOU ARE GOD. As you reflect, imagine, and deepen upon this, you will reconnect and reactivate with the I AM within you, and little by little, your thoughts and words will be blessings of creation for you and your fellow man. The infinite I AM will flow in you, persist and seek it. In the universe, everything is by merit, and nothing happens by chance. Every higher spiritual level reached by other beings has had an evolutionary systematic development process. If you grow and evolve physically, mentally, and spiritually within your free will, your progress is by merit as you sow and develop that growth. The beings with higher spirituality levels have chosen it for themselves, and the basis of this awakening is when they rediscover and reconnect with I GODDESS - I GOD that also dwells in them and you.

There is so much abundance and resources like the numbers 1, 2, 3, 4, 5, 6, 7 to infinity. There are infinite resources for everyone; when you see and hear that there is not, there is little, or it is over, reflect and imagine with your thought the opposite. Remember that whatever you concentrate your thinking on, that is what you will attract. Think and attract that there is an infinity of everything, food, water, oxygen, clothing, joy, peace, happiness, resources, harmony, knowledge, love, health, abundance, wisdom, knowledge, tranquility, security, etc.

Society inserts ideas of scarcity through different educational, governmental, media, etc. When they deprogram you with thoughts of scarcity, they introduce fear to control, manipulate and enslave you. Remember that when you accept fear, you separate yourself from I AM. Fear disappears when you reconnect and rediscover me within you and remember all your infinite potential, I God - I Goddess that dwells within you. I will make you remember the love that you are; as you practice love, fear will disappear as what it always was, an illusion.

Remember that in your being, there is a powerful infinite force; that force is like a muscle that you can exercise and develop. As you exercise it, it will strengthen, grow and expand more and more. In this message lies the information on how to reinforce the reunion with the I God - I Goddess that dwells within you.

## Hey, listen to my voice from within:

## Remember and Know: YOU ARE GOD – YOU ARE GODDESS...

*In several parts of this message, I tell you that you must remember, and I emphasize that because all the knowledge of the universe is in you, you have nothing to learn. Life is not about learning; it is all about remembering. Within you, you carry all the information and knowledge of the universe. Seek me within you, and as you find me, reconnect and reactivate with the I AM, you will commune, remember and have access to the library of knowledge and pure wisdom that dwells within you.*

## Universal Laws of Freedom and Free Will

Our creation is structured by the universal laws of freedom and free will. Watch the birds as they fly and feed freely, without boundaries or barriers; watch the fish as they swim and eat freely in the rivers and seas, without boundaries. Your natural right in this world is to experience freedom and free will in every thought and deed you generate. Feel the oxygen you breathe in and out every moment. When you inhale, oxygen expresses itself freely throughout your world and reaches everyone equally, without discrimination of race, area, or belief. When you inhale and exhale, you know the love that I give to all equally; so is true love, that offers everything and expects nothing in return. The infinite freedom I have given you is like oxygen because it reaches everyone without borders or barriers; it does not ask for anything or demand anything; it simply is. The degree of consciousness and advancement of a society is measured by its inhabitants' freedom and free will. The more unrestricted and responsible they are, the more evolved they will be. Freedom and free will is one of your most sacred essences in this third dimension. **Declare yourself a free and sovereign being.**

Feel and declare yourself free and sovereign, speak it, think it, imagine it, desire it, report it, transmit it, thank it. Decree to the universe: I AM FREE AND SOVEREIGN.

*Remember that in your purest and highest lineage, you were created to be a free and sovereign being; declare it with all the strength of your heart.* ***I AM Free and Sovereign; when you express this, you create freedom and sovereignty***.

I AM the creator of everything visible and invisible in your world, and we created it to be accessible to all, oxygen, water, energy, food, etc. Remember that any resource on the planet belongs to all beings. If you observe that any system of governments, corporations, religions, technologies, businessmen, politicians, scientists, etc., pretend to monopolize a free resource such as water, energy, food, oxygen, etc., you must understand that it is a clear sign that they are violating your free will and freedom. Watch this action because if there is control of these resources, you will end up being a slave to a control system.

Likewise, if you observe that a government, corporation, religion, technology, business, political, scientific, economic, medical or robotic technology, blockchain, digital money, biometrics, digital identification, chips or QR and also for climate issues, etc., try to monopolize or control your freedom and free will, you must understand that it is a clear sign that they intend to violate the right to the natural law of freedom and free will that I AM have granted for all eternity to all beings that inhabit this world. Declare yourself Free and Sovereign: I **AM FREE AND SOVEREIGN.**

You must be attentive to never control, censor, or disqualify your free way of thinking through any media, technological, religious, educational, economic, medical, governmental, scientific, corporate, etc. system. It is very sacred to keep your free thinking; if you lose the freedom to think freely, you will lose the possibility to reunite, reconnect and reactivate with the I AM within you. When you disconnect from the I AM, you become a slave of the implanted system, which will seek by all means to implement a single system of thought based on fear.

If you observe that the current society creates a problem for you and sells you a solution that restricts your privacy and freedom, be cautious and invoke me within you and activate yourself to create reality and enforce your natural right granted by the creator of all that is visible and invisible. Remember that you are free and sovereign and decided to be born here to exercise and live in freedom and free will.

Remember that today's society seeks to control your thinking, inserting false, fictitious, and manipulative feelings, thoughts, and ideas. They want you to think about what they insert to separate you from the I AM that dwells within you. When this happens, you separate yourself from I AM and become easily manipulated, enslaved, controlled, and disconnected from the I AM.

Remember: the most forceful action to influence matter is thought. For this reason, your free thinking is highly sacred because it can create freedom and free will for you and your fellow man. When free thought is blocked, censored, and disqualified, you become a slave to beings with negative energies.

## Science and Pure Knowledge

The science that cannot be questioned or debated is propaganda. The science that does not have an initial cause and effect is false. Your society tells you that some results were obtained through scientific studies to impose them as absolute truths, and you agree with them and accept them as truth. But I tell you that you get a lot of disinformation when they tell you that scientists said this or that; that is why I tell you that you should investigate, question, doubt, reflect, and think about everything they tell you on TV, radio, internet, social networks, artificial intelligence, algorithms, metaverse, holography, virtual reality, etc. Leave behind the mental laziness of believing everything they tell you through these media and question them; questioning is a key that opens the doors to reconnect and reactivate you with the I that dwells in you.

The vast majority of knowledge and information you possess today are ideas, opinions, or unproven theories of other people or organizations, disinformation implanted without logical and rational support.

Often they misinform you with technicalities and fantasies to make you believe it is true, but the major universal truths of the universe are simple and easy to understand. You must believe in your natural and logical observation.

Verify the facts yourselves, question, and rationalize what you see in the media, question what they show you in a photograph or a video, doubt, question, rationalize, reflect, and think. Do not take for truth everything you see on TV, radio, internet, social networks, artificial intelligence, algorithms, metaverse, holography, virtual reality, etc.

Today's technology can create unrealistic fantasies that can be passed off as truth. With technology, they can manipulate and misrepresent any visual, auditory, or sensory content. There are already very advanced software technologies in your world that can create unreal videos and images and pass them off as truth. You see them and accept them as absolute truth, becoming a manipulated, enslaved, and controlled being. Analyze, reflect, question, doubt, investigate and think about all the apparent true information that is inoculated to you by these media. When you seek me within, reconnect, and reactivate with I AM, I will speak to you and show you what is real and false.

The spiritual, mental, and physical advancement of your society will grow to the extent that you question, doubt, investigate, reflect, observe, and analyze every political, medical, economic, social, scientific, food, religious, media, and educational system that governs you now:

Are these systems that make up my society today based on love and seeking the benefit of human beings?

The less you question, reflect, observe, investigate, or think, the more vulnerable you are. True and pure knowledge is achieved by questioning, doubting, and reflecting on everything taught to you by society.

Every human being plays an essential role in the harmony and perfection of the planet. Every thought and feeling affect humanity. Every time you think, your thoughts influence others. **Who can really and truly generate a change in your world is yourself; you have the power and the tools given here, in this message, to do it.**

In the universe, everything is by merit. If you freely choose to reconnect, reactivate, and reunite with I God - I Goddess that I am YOU and dwell in you, I invite you to read and practice this message that is programmed with high-tech codes to activate in your physical, mental, and spiritual body your reconnection and reunification with I Goddess - I God. The time will come if you persist with intuition, courage, focus, love, and faith, where we will be one, and the knowledge and wisdom will come to you from the I God - I Goddess within you. Remember forever that you are my temple.

### Welcome to the NOE: New Spiritual Order.

**The New Spiritual Order (NOE)** is reactivated with this message coming to you and millions of human beings. The NOE is to be aware of the reconnection, reunion, and reactivation of millions of human beings with the I God - I Goddess that lives in each one. It is to have the infallible certainty and knowledge that each human being is responsible for what they create with thought, word, and deed. When millions of human beings rediscover me and commune with the I AM THAT I AM within, your society will evolve to higher dimensions connected by pure love. So be it, and it is.

It is time for you to awaken from your slumber and remember who you are:

**YOU ARE GOD – YOU ARE GODDESS.**

Always For All Eternity, I Will Be For You and In You Waiting For You With Love...

**Genesis 1:26-27**

26. **Then God said, let us make mankind in our image, in our likeness.**

27. **So God created mankind in his own image, in the image of God he created them; male and female he created them.**

Revelation:

26. *Then God and Goddess said, let us make mankind in our image, in our likeness.*

27. *So God and Goddess created mankind in his own image, in the image of God and Goddess he created them; male and female he created them.*

Remember that YOU ARE GOD - YOU ARE GODDESS...

**The True and Real God and Goddess are He and She Who Dwells in You...**

**If you were created in the image and likeness of God and Goddess, what are you?**

**Author:** Elkin Sánchez

To the I AM who dwells in me, I thank you for allowing me to be an instrument of reconnection, reactivation, reunion, and rediscovery of millions of human beings with the God and Goddess that dwells in each one.

I give thanks because every moment I inhale and exhale, I am more aware of you in me and allow you to flow, and we are one.

My greatest desire is to remember the path to align myself with your divine will. Actualize at every instant of the eternal present the information to remember how to find you within me. So be it, and it is.

If you have questions or comments about the message contained in the book, please, contact me through email: youaregods.org@gmail.com

*If you liked the book and it brought knowledge, wisdom and positive experiences to your life, I am infinitely grateful if you can leave a comment or review on Amazon.*

***Invitation:*** If this message vibrated and resonated with you, please share it.

For those people who write to me asking me how they can collaborate to spread the message, here is what I would like to tell you:

1. You can collaborate by reconnecting and reactivating yourself with the God and Goddess that dwells in you; that is enough.

2. If you already feel that you are beginning to reconnect and reactivate with the God-Goddess in you, share the knowledge with other people.

3. Give the book as a gift to others.

4. For those who freely wish to make a voluntary collaboration in money to help expand this knowledge, you can do it through:

**PayPal:** https://www.paypal.com/paypalme/youaregods

**Disclaimer:**

The author makes it known that he has no responsibility to those people who incorrectly transmit or misinterpret the message: You Are God.

The reader is solely responsible for the interpretation and practice of the message.

**Copyright:**

All rights reserved. This book may not be reproduced in whole or in part without written permission from the publisher, except for brief passages in connection with a review; nor way any part of this book be reproduced, stored in a retrieval system, or transmitted in any form or by any means, electronic, mechanical, photocopying, recording, or ther, without written permission fron the publisher.

Copyright© 2022 by Elkin Sánchez

Printed in Great Britain
by Amazon